Cultivate Calm

The Weekly Devotional Study for Multifaceted Christian Women

Theresa Emanuel

Copyright © 2021 Theresa Emanuel

All rights reserved.

ISBN: 9798709960787

DEDICATION

To God be the glory.

CONTENTS

		Acknowledgments	i
		Introduction	Pg #1
		How to Use this Devotional	Pg #5
Part 1 Spirit	Week 1	The blueprint	Pg #11
	Week 2	Created in the image of God	Pg #17
	Week 3	Hope for the future	Pg #21
	Week 4	God's will, will be done	Pg #25
	Week 5	Know your enemy	Pg #29
	Week 6	Makeovers	Pg #33
	Week 7	Faith that pleases God	Pg #37
	Week 8	Be bold with your talent	Pg #41
	Week 9	Walking by faith	Pg #47
	Week 10	Workers with Christ	Pg #51
	Week 11	Mentors	Pg #55
	Week 12	Relax	Pg #59
	Week 13	Prayer of the righteous	Pg #63
	Week 14	An alter ego	Pg #67

	Week 15	Free from fear	Pg #73
	Week 16	God's giving nature	Pg #77
	Week 17	Sharing your light	Pg #81
	Week 18	Rejoice	Pg #85
Part II Mind	Week 19	Words have creative power	Pg #91
	Week 20	Tend and keep	Pg #95
	Week 21	Working as for God	Pg #99
	Week 22	Grow up	Pg #103
	Week 23	Weapons against fear	Pg #107
	Week 24	Lack of knowledge	Pg #111
	Week 25	The power to succeed	Pg #115
	Week 26	Limiting beliefs	Pg #119
	Week 27	Your adversary	Pg #123
	Week 28	Excellence	Pg #127
	Week 29	Tithing	Pg #131
	Week 30	Walk in the path created	Pg #137
	Week 31	Filled with creativity	Pg #141

Cultivate Calm: The Weekly Devotional Study for Multifaceted Christian Women

	Week 32	God is faithful	Pg #145
	Week 33	Don't quit	Pg #149
	Week 34	Bold thoughts and actions	Pg #153
	Week 35	Personal experience	Pg #157
	Week 36	Simplify	Pg #163
Part III Body	Week 37	Your body is holy	Pg #169
	Week 38	Physical senses	Pg #173
	Week 39	Fellowship	Pg #177
	Week 40	Fear and health	Pg #181
	Week 41	Christ magnified in your body	Pg #185
	Week 42	Peace and healing	Pg #189
	Week 43	What to eat	Pg #193
	Week 44	Body image	Pg #197
	Week 45	Faith and your body	Pg #201
	Week 46	Pain	Pg #205
	Week 47	Physical fitness	Pg #209
	Week 48	Boldly break bread	Pg #213
	Week 49	Nothing to wear	Pg #217

Week 50	Prosperity of the body	Pg #221
Week 51	Exercise	Pg #225
Week 52	Age joyfully	Pg #229
	Conclusion	Pg #233
	About the author	Pg #235

ACKNOWLEDGMENTS

My darling husband Chris, you have my love and admiration. You amaze me with your wisdom and understanding of the human condition. I appreciate the love and support you provide as I let my many facets sparkle.

My parents, I love you and thank you for giving birth to me and introducing me to the love of God. You instilled in me an enduring desire for learning which helped to make this book possible.

My book coach, Kathy Miles Wheeler, you have my sincere appreciation and thanks. Your coaching helps others to shine their lights. Your abilities to instruct, encourage and prod were necessary for this book to make it from an idea to a tangible creation I can now hold in my hand.

My lifelong friends and cheerleaders, you have my love and gratitude. I treasure our fellowship as it allows us to share the best of ourselves in our many roles. Most notably, Jacquelyn Hatch, Dr. Darlene Dockery, and Yvette Tilghman, I thank you for your constant reassurance of the need for such a book and your requests for the finished product. You helped me stay faithful on the days that the work was a struggle.

Rev. Dr. Barbara Heck, thank you for lessons in storytelling and thought-provoking questions on living our faith. These lessons help me to be bold in sharing the Good News with others.

You, dear reader, thank you for embarking on this journey to grow in peace, calm, and radiance.

INTRODUCTION

Theresa Emanuel

INTRODUCTION

This devotional study is for busy Christian women who seek God first. Stop the overwhelm and disheartenment from feeling like you're chasing too many opportunities. God knows that you are a multi-purposed, multi-passionate, and multi-talented creature with a tripartite nature to nurture. Yes, you have multiple roles to fill and many passions you want to pursue. God created you in His multifaceted image, meaning this is only natural. His Word holds the key to a successful, calm, fulfilled life with all your facets glowing in splendor.

You have a tripartite nature designed to work in harmony. Your spirit allows you to communicate with God and draw your strength from abiding in Him. You have to lean on God to do that which you cannot. When you do, you can walk in the peace of the knowledge of your calling. Your mind allows you to do your part for the kingdom of God. It's the part of you that creates and reasons. Your body is the vehicle that enables you to function in this realm. It needs to be well maintained for you to achieve your many goals. I believe God wants us to live and pursue our passions from a place of calm and peace rather than overwhelm.

This devotional study will meet you where you are in your life, relationships, and business. These lessons and prayers will help you receive God's love and blessings without guilt or fear. Find calm and peace while fulfilling the roles and duties of your multifaceted life. You will be encouraged to be courageous through the increased knowledge of God and the knowledge of yourself. You will gain the discipline to be obedient in your health and self-care. Your work ethic and finances will be Word driven. Learn to speak God's truth in your self-talk, relationships, and business dealings. Prosperity and success will be the outcome of the daily patterns and habits laid out in this book. Use this devotional to improve your relationship with Father God, and then let Him improve you and your relationships with others.

HOW TO USE THIS DEVOTIONAL

Theresa Emanuel

HOW TO USE THIS DEVOTIONAL

There are various ways to use this book. Regardless of the method you select, freely write in this devotional, dog-ear the pages, and take pictures of your favorite sections for easy reference. There are three sections: spirit, mind, and body. Option one goes straight through the book from week one to week 52. However, if you want to nurture each part of your tripartite nature on a monthly basis, visit calm.p31virtues.com for access to an outline of this option. This website also includes access to a third option, which is a theme-based schedule. As always, trust the Holy Spirit for guidance on how to use this devotional.

Each week includes a scripture from the New King James Version of the Bible, a lesson, a prayer, confession, journal prompts in the delve deeper sections, along with suggestions for creating, building habits, and putting your faith into action. This book is unique because its design allows you to ask God for guidance, affirm His Word over your life, and accomplish your goals by following His will. The constructive journaling will help you reflect more intentionally. Express your creativity via works of art in addition to creating a calm and beautiful lifestyle of walking daily with God. Go deep into the scripture and make it real in your everyday life by changing your habits and putting your faith into action.

Each week includes a habit suggestion. However, studies show that it takes 21 to 30 days to build a new habit. Therefore, if you find a practice is working for you, feel free to stick with that habit for the next three weeks rather than work on a new one. A few fundamental lifestyle changes built during the year will effectively create calm.

Finally, I am here for you for the next 52 weeks and beyond. As you go through the process of cultivating calm, reach out to me at theresa@p31virtues.com or set up a time to chat using the link at calm.p31virtues.com. Share your creative works by tagging me on Instagram @p31virtues with the hashtag #multifacetedp31women. I pray that God will bless you as you move forward and experience calm in your faith and all aspects of your multifaceted life.

PART ONE
SPIRIT

WEEK 1
THE BLUEPRINT

Joshua 1:3-9

Every place that the sole of your foot will tread upon I have given you, as I said to Moses. [4] From the wilderness and this Lebanon as far as the great river, the River Euphrates, all the land of the Hittites, and to the Great Sea toward the going down of the sun, shall be your territory. [5] No man shall be able to stand before you all the days of your life; as I was with Moses, so I will be with you. I will not leave you nor forsake you. [6] Be strong and of good courage, for to this people you shall divide as an inheritance the land which I swore to their fathers to give them. [7] Only be strong and very courageous, that you may observe to do according to all the law which Moses My servant commanded you; do not turn from it to the right hand or to the left, that you may prosper wherever you go. [8] This Book of the Law shall not depart from your mouth, but you shall meditate in it day and night, that you may observe to do according to all that is written in it. For then you will make your way prosperous, and then you will have good success. ⁹ Have I not commanded you? Be strong and of good courage; do not be afraid, nor be dismayed, for the Lord your God is with you wherever you go."

The blueprint

This scripture is a blueprint for success in your calling. First, God is saying that He has already given it to you. You only need to take the steps. God will be with you and will not leave you. No man will be able to prevent what God has ordained. Obey the command to be passionate and courageous. God repeats the directive three times, so it must be important. Obey God's Word meditate on God's Word, be a doer of God's Word. Then you will be prosperous, and you will have success in every aspect of life.

Will describes an inevitable event. It is God's will for those who are obedient to His Word to be successful. God's will comes to pass. So do your part in bringing His will to manifestation.

Don't get sidetracked. There are so many distractions in today's world. It's easy to get off track from the purpose God has put on your heart. Weakness, fear, and man are the things that will get you off track. Weakness or lacking steadfastness will make you give up just short of your goal. Fear can prevent you from even getting started. Man can coax you into activities that do not propel you in the right direction.

But God is for you. Heed the whisper of the Holy Spirit and stay on track. Be obedient, courageous, and committed. He said you could, so if you will, then you will experience the blessings promised.

Pray

Heavenly Father, forgive me when I get sidetracked from the calling you have placed on my life. Thank you for your promise and your anointing. Please keep me ever mindful of your promise, my purpose and my obligation to do your will. I thank you and praise you for my good success. In Jesus' name, amen.

Read and Confess

Read: Psalm 40:8
Confess: I delight to do Your will, O my God,
And Your law *is* within my heart.

Delve Deeper

How do you define courage and in what ways do you display that courage?

_____
_____
_____
_____
_____
_____
_____
_____
_____
_____
_____
_____
_____
_____
_____

Delve Deeper

What prevents you from being steadfast in your calling?

_____
_____
_____
_____
_____
_____
_____
_____
_____
_____
_____
_____
_____

Create

Create a top three list of tasks essential to achieving your primary calling.

Build a Habit

Set a clear intention for each day this week.

Put Faith into Action

Say no to activities that don't serve your primary purpose.

WEEK 2
CREATED IN THE IMAGE OF GOD

Genesis 1:26-27

Then God said, "Let Us make man in Our image, according to Our likeness; let them have dominion over the fish of the sea, over the birds of the air, and over the cattle, over all the earth and over every creeping thing that creeps on the earth." 27 So God created man in His own image; in the image of God He created him; male and female He created them.

Created in the image of God

As a human creature, you are the image of God. Therefore it's no surprise that you are multi-passionate, multi-talented, and multi-focused. Just as God is tripartite, you are tripartite. God is Father, Son, and Spirit, and you are Spirit, Mind, and Body. Each part serves a specific function, and each component steps forward or back as needed.

When preparing my speaker biography, my coach advised that it would be confusing for others if I listed more than three roles that I fill. Sometimes it seems as if the world is trying to restrain us or put us in a box. Then we turn around and put ourselves in a box, taking common ideas and limiting ourselves. We tell ourselves to tamp it down, remove some of our flavors, and zest to make ourselves more palatable for others. Then we wonder why we feel a void. In reality, this denies the world of our purpose, the exact purpose God created us to fulfill.

Be satisfied. Focus on who you are as a creature in the image of God. Pray that the Holy Spirit will put you into remembrance of your role and purpose any time someone or something causes you to consider taking a step back from the greatness for which He created you.

Pray

Dear Father, forgive me for putting limits on myself based on the world's view of me. Thank you for the multifaceted woman you created me to be. Help me to embrace all of me and share myself with the world so that I may bring glory to you. In Jesus' name, amen.

Confess

I am created in God's image.

Delve Deeper

What characteristics did you have as a child that you still embrace today?

_____
_____
_____
_____
_____
_____

Delve Deeper

What is an area of influence that God has entrusted to you?

Create

Create a self-portrait.

Build a Habit

This week smile at yourself when you look in the mirror.

Put Faith into Action

Be a responsible consumer this week.

WEEK 3
HOPE FOR THE FUTURE

Jeremiah 29:11
For I know the thoughts that I think toward you, says the Lord, thoughts of peace and not of evil, to give you a future and a hope.

Hope for the future

Jeremiah 29:11 was written to Israel when they were in bondage in Babylon for 70 years. God was promising that He was not abandoning them in their situation. God's promise to Christians is even better. The book of John tells us that the thief comes to kill, steal, and destroy. Christ came to give us abundant life. You can hope or trust God's plan even if you don't feel close to Him at present.

As a child, I was going to bed late. Consequently, my mother revoked my television privileges. Outraged over the punishment, I entered the house without talking. When my mother questioned my silence, I yelled, I don't speak to people I don't like! This behavior did not restore my television privileges. Yet, it did not revoke the protection my parents provided. I had the same shelter, food, and clothing. I share that story to remind you that despite any emotion you have, you are God's child. That emotion will not cause Him to withhold any provisions He has for you. If you have anger, frustration, or sadness, it's okay. If you have joy and happiness, give glory to God.

No matter where you are in life, there is hope for your future. God is not surprised by where you are or your response to your circumstances. However, He wants you to focus on Him rather than your circumstances. Stay connected with God spiritually. Keep your focus on Him. It's the only way to experience the plans He has for you.

Pray

Father in Heaven, forgive me when I lash out at you or question the plan you have for my life. Thank you for the thoughts you have towards me. Teach me to let your thoughts be my thoughts and to hope, trust and live the glorious life you have planned for me. In Jesus' name, amen.

Read and Confess

Read: Ephesians 3:20-21
Confess: God can do above any of my hopes.

Delve Deeper

What evidence do you have that God loves you when you're at your worst?

_____

_____

_____

Delve Deeper

How do you show thanks to God for the blessings you have while you strive to fulfill the hopes He has for you?

_____

_____

_____

_____

_____

_____

_____

Create

Create a calendar showing the dates on which you will accomplish something God has planned for you.

Build a habit

Before you commit to an obligation, be sure it is in line with the hopes God has for you.

Put Faith into Action

Take action toward accomplishing a dream God has given you.

WEEK 4
GOD'S WILL, WILL BE DONE

Psalm 46:10

Be still, and know that I am God; I will be exalted among the nations, I will be exalted in the earth

God's will, will be done

For a second-grade Sunday school lesson, the class did a puzzle. Students had to find hidden puzzle pieces. Then each student put their piece on a felt board to complete the puzzle. One of the students was nervous. She didn't want to place her puzzle piece on the board. I explained to her that we couldn't complete the puzzle without her piece. We needed her participation. In the end, I placed her piece for her.

God's will manifests. His plan will occur with or without you. God created you for a purpose as part of His master plan. Take the opportunity to lean into your God-given talent. Fulfill the purpose God created for you. Don't allow Him to find someone else to fulfill your role.

Know that Father God can and will do it without you but He doesn't want to. It's a gift and a blessing to be allowed to participate in the plan Father God has for us and the world.

Pray

Father in Heaven, forgive me when I shy away from my calling. Thank you for allowing me to be a part of your plan for the world. Help me to be bold and participate as you have called me. In Jesus' name, amen.

Read and Confess

Read: Hebrews 13:20-21
Confess: I am complete and have everything I need to do God's will.

Delve Deeper

Can you think of a time when you were called to do something but shied away? What was the outcome?

_____
_____
_____
_____
_____
_____
_____
_____
_____
_____

Delve Deeper

What is Father God currently calling you to do?

Create

Create a mission statement for your life or business.

Build a Habit

This week let go of any assumptions you may have about other people or topics.

Put Faith into Action

Today when you get a nudge from the Holy Spirit to take an action, take it immediately.

WEEK 5
KNOW YOUR ENEMY

Ephesians 6:12

For we do not wrestle against flesh and blood, but against principalities, against powers, against the rulers of the darkness of this age, against spiritual hosts of wickedness in the heavenly places.

Know your enemy

You have the power to overcome the enemy. God has given you His weapons and strength to be victorious. When you feel like stepping back, be sure the enemy is not trying to stifle you. It is critical to recognize the real enemy.

It can be so tempting to blame other people for the things that annoy us. Situations that keep us from wanting to share the best of ourselves. I am a member of a community service organization. One evening I was working on a committee with a dear friend of mine. Over dinner, she expressed her frustration with another committee member. My friend explained how another member was impeding her enjoyment of working in the group. I reminded her of this scripture. I didn't think the person mentioned was the problem—who was she to have such power? I encouraged my friend to pray for the woman when she felt frustrated. Pray that God would bless this person. My friend thought that it might be deceitful to do this. I encouraged her to consider it an act of obedience. It would help her change her thinking in this area.

The enemy is real and will use others to work against us. Be strong; use the spiritual weapons of God. You have the weapons of prayer and the Word.

Pray

Dear Lord, forgive me for using others as an excuse to not share the gifts you've given me. Thank you for your Word and prayer to use as weapons against my real enemy. Please help me to heed the nudge of the Holy Spirit to pray and act on your Word. In Jesus' name, amen.

Read and Confess

Read: Psalm 29:11

Confess: The Lord will give strength to me and bless me with peace.

Delve Deeper

What additional knowledge of God would increase your ability to do His will?

_____

_____

_____

_____

Delve Deeper

How will your life improve if you rely more on prayer and the Word?

_____

_____

_____

_____

_____

_____

_____

Create

Create a keychain to remind yourself that you hold the key and the authority.

Build a Habit

Pray non-stop each day this week.

Put Faith into Action

This week pray daily for someone you think causes you stress or frustration.

WEEK 6
MAKEOVERS

Psalm 100:3

Know that the Lord, He is God; It is He who has made us, and not we ourselves; we are His people and the sheep of His pasture.

Makeovers

Get to know the Lord so you can know yourself. Who we are is defined by whose we are. Christians do not need to be self-made. That is a trait of the world. If we want to have the peace of God, we have to know that we are His making. God will continue the creation if we let Him. Going out and doing things by ourselves only results in frustration and stress.

Do not move forward in any way to make yourself over. God, who created you, will perform the makeover. Your part involves learning, understanding, and living accordingly. Resist the pull of the world by staying grounded in the Word of God. Use the Bible to help prioritize your life. Your heart will be more Christ-like, improving your ability to empathize with others. The self-knowledge gained will increase self-control. The peace you gain will be energizing and increase your joy.

As a child of God, you do not have to worry about success. On a deeper level, you do not have to worry about who you want to be on your way to success. God has defined it all for you. Look to the Word for your values and to the Holy Spirit for the inspiration and wisdom needed for victory.

Pray

Heavenly Father, please absolve my sin of trying to be self-made. Thank you for the miraculous way in which I was created and for continuing to shape and mold me. Help me to do my part to learn, understand and live according to your Word. In Jesus' name, amen.

Read and Confess

Read: Psalm 119:66
Confess: God will teach me good judgment and knowledge.

Delve Deeper

What knowledge do you want to gain and develop?

_____
_____
_____
_____
_____
_____
_____
_____

Delve Deeper

What areas of your life is God currently making over?

_____

_____

_____

Create

Create a message board to post things you want to learn.

Build a Habit

Listen to others fully when you're communicating this week.

Put Faith into Action

Let go and let God. Stop trying to do work that only God can do.

WEEK 7
FAITH THAT PLEASES GOD

Hebrews 11:6

But without faith it is impossible to please Him, for he who comes to God must believe that He is, and that He is a rewarder of those who diligently seek Him.

Faith that pleases God

I have met people who believe in their salvation but fail to trust God in other aspects of life. I assume that if you are reading this, you are a born again believer in Father God and Jesus Christ. Therefore you believe that He is. You are confident of the resurrection and where you will spend eternity. Be equally assured in His ability to help you succeed in your business and your desires in life.

This verse should reassure you that God is a rewarder. A rewarder of those who diligently seek Him. Seek Him, not success, not more clients, not the perfect space, perfect logo, perfect whatever aspect of your life or business you are currently stressing over. Seek Him and let Him guide you. You will know what to do next, but you will have to take the actions to do it.

Faith is not praying and sitting and watching. Hopeful confidence is seeking and listening and doing. It is acting despite the difficulties and maybe despite what others say. It is not dependent on what our physical senses tell us or what our university-educated brain tells us. It's action on the knowledge imparted by the Holy Spirit. So commune and listen and obey and act and reap the reward that God has for you.

Pray

Heavenly Father, forgive me when I doubt your ability or desire to help me succeed in life and business. Thank you for the wisdom you provide through the Holy Spirit. Please give me ears to hear and help me put my faith into action so that I may reap the reward you have for me. In Jesus' name, amen.

Read and Confess

Read: Psalm 70:4

Confess: I rejoice and am glad in the Lord because I seek Him.

Delve Deeper

In what ways are you diligently seeking God?

_____

_____

_____

_____

_____

_____

_____

Delve Deeper

Is there something that the Holy Spirit has been prompting you to do but you have not done yet? What is holding you back from taking that action?

_____

_____

_____

_____

_____

Create

Create a profile or bio to help you connect with like-minded people.

Build a Habit

Before you get out of bed each day this week, pray.

Put Faith into Action

Take a baby step in the direction that you are being prompted in by the Holy Spirit.

WEEK 8
BE BOLD WITH YOUR TALENT

Matthew 25:14-30

"For the kingdom of heaven is like a man traveling to a far country, who called his own servants and delivered his goods to them. [15] And to one he gave five talents, to another two, and to another one, to each according to his own ability; and immediately he went on a journey. [16] Then he who had received the five talents went and traded with them, and made another five talents. [17] And likewise he who had received two gained two more also. [18] But he who had received one went and dug in the ground, and hid his lord's money. [19] After a long time the lord of those servants came and settled accounts with them. [20] "So he who had received five talents came and brought five other talents, saying, 'Lord, you delivered to me five talents; look, I have gained five more talents besides them.'[21] His lord said to him, 'Well done, good and faithful servant; you were faithful over a few things, I will make you ruler over many things. Enter into the joy of your lord.'[22] He also who had received two talents came and said,

'Lord, you delivered to me two talents; look, I have gained two more talents besides them.' [23] His lord said to him, 'Well done, good and faithful servant; you have been faithful over a few things, I will make you ruler over many things. Enter into the joy of your lord.' [24] "Then he who had received the one talent came and said, 'Lord, I knew you to be a hard man, reaping where you have not sown, and gathering where you have not scattered seed. [25] And I was afraid, and went and hid your talent in the ground. Look, there you have what is yours.' [26] "But his lord answered and said to him, 'You wicked and lazy servant, you knew that I reap where I have not sown, and gather where I have not scattered seed. [27] So you ought to have deposited my money with the bankers, and at my coming I would have received back my own with interest. [28] So take the talent from him, and give it to him who has ten talents. [29] 'For to everyone who has, more will be given, and he will have abundance; but from him who does not have, even what he has will be taken away. [30] And cast the unprofitable servant into the outer darkness. There will be weeping and gnashing of teeth.'

Be bold with your talent

Early in my career as a dentist, I was talking with a friend who said he thought most people were wasting their talents. I found this hard to believe since I was new, eager, and ready to share my skills with the world. Many years later, I think he was right. Today I enjoy meeting new dentists because the shiny newness is so apparent and radiant in them. We must pray for this spark and fight to keep it.

Faith requires us to be bold and to take risks. Boldness is magic. It is the magic that children believe in, seize, and manipulate. Father God has given you your talent based on your ability. The servant with the one talent lost everything. The thing that he feared, losing the funds, came to pass. God has provided an environment for us to succeed, so move forward boldly. Ask "what if it's a success," rather than "what if I fail."

Hold on to your child-like boldness by keeping the spark of enthusiasm alive for your passion. Don't get comfortable where you are such that you don't move forward. Pretend you're just beginning and see how much further you can go. Remember your purpose and whom you serve. If you've found your talent, be bold with it. Use it. Press on even when it may seem as though things are going downhill. Father God knows the difficulties you will face, and He will see you through them. Celebrate every small win and keep pressing forward.

Pray

Heavenly Father, forgive me for the temptation to bury my talent. Thank you for providing me my talent according to my ability. Please help me to be bold in sharing my talent in a way that is pleasing to you. In Jesus' name, amen.

Read and Confess

Read: Psalm 138:3
Confess: God will embolden me when I call on Him.

Delve Deeper

When have you been courageous?

_____

_____

_____

_____

_____

_____

Delve Deeper

How would you like to spend your last day in this realm?

_____
_____
_____
_____
_____

Create

Create an accomplishment board.

Build a Habit

This week choose the options that push you beyond your comfort zone.

Put Faith into Action

Give a compliment to a stranger.

WEEK 9
WALKING BY FAITH

2 Corinthians 5:7
For we walk by faith, not by sight.

Walking by faith

So many times, when we get discouraged, it is because of our physical circumstances. Our walk is one of faith and not one based on our physical senses. If our purpose and mission are God-given, then the outcome is beyond this physical realm, and we can rely on Father God to bring to pass that which He promised. To look at the physical circumstance and become doubtful is an act of disobedience.

We like to pencil out a plan for the future and factor in the current situation. We call it being realistic, but we may be putting limits on the unlimited power of God. We can only receive those blessings that we believe. We look at the lives of others, and then claim their testimonies as our own. We do this even when their situation is not the life to which we aspire. When what you are working so earnestly to accomplish seems to be continuously derailed, check in with the

Father. Ask and confirm that it is His will for you. If it is His will, then trust that what you're going through is preparation for the manifestation of your desire.

Keep your eyes on the vision that Father God gave you. Believe in His ability to bring it to pass as you do your part. Be steadfast in your walk of faith.

Pray

Heavenly Father, forgive me when I base my beliefs and future on what I see around me. I praise you for the vision you have given me for my life. Help me to stay in tune with your Spirit when I get discouraged so that I may stay strong in my faith for all that you have planned for me. In Jesus' name, amen.

Confess

My hopes endure all circumstances.

Delve Deeper

How can you be happy for others who receive a blessing for which you've been praying?

_____
_____
_____
_____
_____
_____
_____

Delve Deeper

How can you be more forgiving of yourself?

_____

_____

_____

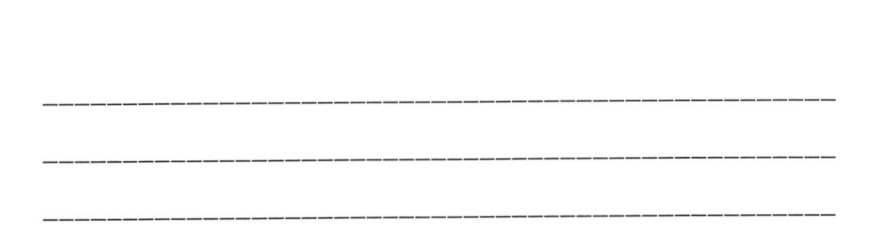

Create

Create a playlist of uplifting songs.

Build a Habit

This week be aware of the Holy Spirit every time you move from one location to another.

Put Faith into Action

Show up with expectation at the next worship service or Bible study you attend.

WEEK 10
WORKERS WITH CHRIST

1 Corinthians 3:6-8

I planted, Apollos watered, but God gave the increase. [7] So then neither he who plants is anything, nor he who waters, but God who gives the increase. [8] Now he who plants and he who waters are one, and each one will receive his own reward according to his own labor.

Workers with Christ

In God's structure, everyone has a role to play. The final product doesn't happen if there is a part undone, making everyone essential. Success is based on accomplishing the total job.

My husband and I work together in our real estate business. I focus on finding the property and setting the offer details. My husband focuses on getting the property rented. Yet it's one business, and we are one as husband and wife. We are not in competition with each other or anyone else. We profit based on how well we each perform our roles. Along the way, other people benefit, depending on their part in the project. Since we take on a lot of the risk, we receive a lot of the reward. Yet other people such as the realtor, title company, construction company, handyman, and other businesspeople receive pay and profit for their work on the property. It would be inefficient and less than profitable for us to take on the duties of these vendors. Additionally, that is not where we find the joy of real estate. Success comes from everyone doing what they enjoy and do best.

The same is true in our work for the kingdom of God. Focus on the assignment Father God has given to you. Do not feel as though you compete with anyone for profit. God will bring all the pieces together for the accomplishment of His plan. Working together with God ensures success.

Pray

Father in Heaven, forgive me when I set myself in competition with my brothers and sisters in Christ. Thank You for giving each of us roles that we enjoy to help in the fulfillment of your plan. Help me to stay focused on my assignment so that I may better serve you. In Jesus' name, amen.

Read and Confess

Read: Proverbs 16:3
Confess: God is in charge of my work, and my plans succeed.

Delve Deeper

What would you like to have said at your 99th birthday party and by whom?

_____

_____

_____

___

Delve Deeper
What distractions are you allowing to affect your success?
___

_____

_____

_____

_____

_____

_____

_____

_____

Create

Create a going and coming station in your home for keys, coats, and bags.

Build a Habit

Start saving regularly or increase your regular savings.

Put Faith into Action

Pray for someone you consider or used to consider the competition.

WEEK 11
MENTORS

John 14:16
And I will pray the Father, and He will give you another Helper, that He may abide with you forever—

Mentors

People are encouraged to get a mentor when they are starting anything new. The mentor is someone who is at or has been where they want to go. The Holy Spirit has been everywhere and is all knowing and is a great mentor to consult. Before starting anything, small or large, be sure to consult with your best advisor, the Holy Spirit. Then seek His counsel on who to seek instruction from in the natural realm as you move forward.

In my experience, the advice I receive from others is more a reflection of them than my situation or the best path forward. Be sure to consider the knowledge and information you receive to pick the pearl of wisdom that is right for you. Look for the advice that comes multiple times. Confirmation from two or three witnesses. Your mother may ask about the project you started and then set aside, then the next day, a friend may ask the same question, later you may see something on social media that directly correlates with the project. God is trying to tell you something, pick up that project, and get to work.

Start each day and work session with prayer and ask for guidance. The Holy Spirit offers an easier way to accomplish your goal. Stop trying to do it alone; receive His offer.

Pray

Heavenly Father, forgive me when I fail to seek the Holy Spirit as my first mentor. Thank you for such an amazing helper. Teach me to fully utilize this resource to succeed beyond my wildest dream and bring glory to you. In Jesus' name, amen.

Read and Confess

Read: 1 Corinthians 2:12

Confess: I know the things God has freely given to me because I have received the Holy Spirit.

Delve Deeper

How does the counsel of the Holy Spirit affect you and your work?

_____

_____

_____

_____

_____

_____

_____
_____
_____
_____
_____
_____
_____
_____

Delve Deeper

Write about an area where you have been nudged three or more times.

_____
_____
_____
_____
_____
_____
_____
_____
_____
_____
_____

_____

_____

_____

_____

Create

Create an agenda and three specific questions to ask your earthly mentor.

Build a Habit

Share your hopes with someone close to you who will hold you accountable.

Put Faith into Action

Start each day, each project, and each action you take this week by praying, "Father, please help me."

WEEK 12
RELAX

Philippians 4:7
... and the peace of God, which surpasses all understanding, will guard your hearts and minds through Christ Jesus.

Relax

We are most productive from a place of peace and tranquility. God's Word tells us that we have the peace of God, and He guards our hearts and minds. In my study of biology, I learned that God created our cell receptors to be active in a relaxed state. I believe that this is the way God made our entire being. Therefore, we can move forward and function in the world while in a relaxed state.

In your business and your life, you should know that God is your source. Operating from this state of calm will improve your results. No one likes high-pressure tactics in sales or life. Guards go up when pressured to make purchases or take action. There is a real stench emitted from someone pushy. Forceful people stop seeing the person they're talking with and see only the end or the gaining of their desires. When information is imparted and offers given to be taken or left, the hearer is more likely to perceive that you care. The receiver can then objectively weigh your offer without being run off by a horrific odor.

Be at peace. Rely on your creator and trust the way your system and spiritual laws can work for you. Relax, be ready, and be receptive. You are most effective in an untroubled state of being.

Pray

Heavenly Father, forgive me when I get stressed and rob myself of peace by not relying on you. Thank you for creating me to lean on you and have the ability to function from a place of peace. Help me to use this knowledge to better serve others. In Jesus' name, amen.

Read and Confess

Read: Isaiah 9:6
Confess: I have peace in Christ.

Delve Deeper

What do you dream of doing but have not done?

_____
_____
_____
_____
_____
_____
_____

Delve Deeper

Write about a moment in your life that you'd like to relive.

_____

_____

_____

Create

Create a bucket list for the current season.

Build a Habit

Listen to Christian music this week.

Put Faith into Action

Take on a challenging project or activity that causes you to expand or improve your abilities.

WEEK 13
PRAYER OF THE RIGHTEOUS

James 5:16

Confess your trespasses to one another, and pray for one another, that you may be healed. The effective, fervent prayer of a righteous man avails much.

Prayer of the righteous

I was in Baltimore, leaving the pharmacy at Johns Hopkins Hospital. There was a woman with a hood seemingly created from a blanket, holding a cup begging. Her beauty was stunning and there was a tentative sweetness to her manner. I took some money from my cup holder and rolled down my window. Handing her the money, I said, I give this to you in Jesus' name. She smiled, saying thank you. Then she said, pray for me. Surprised by that response, I smiled, nodding, and replied, yes, I will. Yet in the back of mind, I was thinking, doesn't she know she can pray for herself?

When I returned home, I shared the experience and my thoughts with my husband. He said, of course she knows, she can pray for herself, but she sees you in your condition and herself in hers. Then he presented this scripture as the rationale for her request.

I'm thankful for my husband and his wisdom in breaking down the explanation of the situation in such a loving way. My trespass was trivializing or questioning the appeal. Don't wait for severe circumstances to go to God in prayer. Know the power of prayer. Pray for yourself, pray for others, and ask others to pray for you.

Pray

Father in Heaven, please forgive me when I hesitate to go to you in prayer. Thank you for your Word and the knowledge of the power of the prayer of the righteous. Help me to utilize this power daily to benefit your kingdom. In Jesus' name, amen.

Read and Confess

Read: 2 Corinthians 5:21

Confess: I am the righteousness of God in Jesus Christ, and my prayers are profitable.

Delve Deeper

When did you hesitate to take action but then were glad that you did act?

_____

_____

_____

_____

_____

_____

_____

Delve Deeper
What skills do you have today that you didn't have last year?

_____

_____

_____

_____

Create
Create a prayer journal.

Build a Habit
This week ask for help when you need it.

Put Faith into Action
Pray.

WEEK 14
AN ALTER EGO

Proverbs 31:15-28

She also rises while it is yet night,
And provides food for her household,
And a portion for her maidservants.
[16] She considers a field and buys it;
From her profits she plants a vineyard.
[17] She girds herself with strength,
And strengthens her arms.
[18] She perceives that her merchandise is good,
And her lamp does not go out by night.
[19] She stretches out her hands to the distaff,
And her hand holds the spindle.
[20] She extends her hand to the poor,
Yes, she reaches out her hands to the needy.
[21] She is not afraid of snow for her household,
For all her household is clothed with scarlet.
[22] She makes tapestry for herself;

Her clothing is fine linen and purple.
²³ Her husband is known in the gates,
When he sits among the elders of the land.
²⁴ She makes linen garments and sells them,
And supplies sashes for the merchants.
²⁵ Strength and honor are her clothing;
She shall rejoice in time to come.
²⁶ She opens her mouth with wisdom,
And on her tongue is the law of kindness.
²⁷ She watches over the ways of her household,
And does not eat the bread of idleness.
²⁸ Her children rise up and call her blessed;
Her husband also, and he praises her:

An Alter Ego

Do you admire the Proverbs 31 woman or look at her with disdain for setting impossible expectations? If you are a Christian female, you have it in you to be a Proverbs 31 woman. Learn to follow in her footsteps. She can teach you how to maximize your talent, treasure, and time.

Her skills include developing a niche, doing due diligence, and negotiating. She creates a moneymaking machine. Then, using the profits, she purchases a vineyard, another moneymaking machine. Managing her profits includes being generous and giving to the poor. Money management includes having an emergency fund. She knows how to make her money work for her.

When money works for you, you can maximize your time and spend it with your family. Use your time wisely. Get up early. Know the importance of good food for your family and yourself. Delegate tasks to a virtual assistant or a vendor to free up time. Then take care of these people. Show them respect, and ensure they are well paid.

Use the Proverb 31 woman as a model to make the most of your talent, money, and time. Lean into this woman, embrace her as an alter ego. It wouldn't be in the book if it were unattainable.

Pray

Heavenly Father, forgive me when I fight or become frustrated by the expectations you have for me. Thank you for high standards and blueprints to achieve them. Show me the version of the Proverbs 31 woman you created me to be. Help me to blossom into the fullness of that creation. In Jesus' name, amen.

Confess

I am exemplary in my many roles as a woman, daughter, sister, wife, mother, friend, homemaker, employee, and entrepreneur.

Delve Deeper

What aspects of the Proverbs 31 woman come most easily for you?

_____
_____
_____
_____
_____
_____
_____
_____
_____
_____

Delve Deeper

What other aspects of the Proverbs 31 woman is the Holy Spirit nudging you to embrace?

_____

_____

_____

Create

Create spare time by delegating a task.

Build a Habit

Read Mark 12:30-31 and meditate on it daily this week.

Put Faith into Action

Read the Word out loud this week.

WEEK 15
FREE FROM FEAR

Romans 8:15

For you did not receive the spirit of bondage again to fear, but you received the Spirit of adoption by whom we cry out, "Abba, Father."

Free from fear

Fear is due to a belief about one's circumstances. Because we believe in the living God, we are free from fear. We do not walk based on our natural situations. Our spiritual condition confirms our relationship as children of God. He desires to include us in what He is building.

In the classic movie, the *Godfather*, the Godfather solves problems and fears. The Godfather has biological sons, Sonny, Fredo, and Michael. He also has a son, Tom, who he took in and raised as one of the family. Tom went to school and had a place in the family business. Tom states that Pop was just as much a father to him as he was to Sonny.

God is just as much a father to you as He is to Christ. When you know who you are, you don't have to be afraid. You can live in the joy of the promise of salvation. Connect and commune with God. Get excited about the vision God has given you. Embrace every aspect of your multifaceted life. You were born again to work with God and be a part of the family business. Wake up every morning excited to participate in what God is creating, in you and through you.

Pray

Heavenly Father, forgive me when I act like I'm not a member of your family. Thank you for taking me in and including me and allowing me to work with you in your creation. Help me to remember the support I have as a member of the family and that I never need to fear. In Jesus' name, amen.

Read and Confess

Read: Psalm 34:4
Confess: I am free from fear because I seek the Lord.

Delve Deeper

What frightens you? Is that fear keeping you safe or holding you back?

_____
_____
_____
_____
_____
_____
_____

Delve Deeper

What desire of yours do you think God may take or not provide?

_____

_____

_____

_____

Create

Create an essential oil blend or find a fragrance that helps you relax.

Build a habit

When you have a task that frightens you, accomplish it immediately to prevent fear from increasing.

Put Faith into Action

This week do or take a step toward doing something that frightens you.

WEEK 16
GOD'S GIVING NATURE

Matthew 7:11

If you then, being evil, know how to give good gifts to your children, how much more will your Father who is in heaven give good things to those who ask Him!

God's giving nature

The best gift-givers enjoy giving. A good gift-giver knows the receiver and makes the gift personal to them. They give gifts that remind the recipient of the giver and the giver's love for them. They decide what gift will provide value and gratification without regard to the price tag. Lower priced gifts may show more compassion and understanding of the receiver. Yet a high price gift could let the recipient have something they want but wouldn't splurge on for themself. Good gift-givers take risks. They may give a gift the recipient has never experienced; yet the giver believes the receiver will find benefit and enjoyment from the present.

Father God is the best gift-giver. God planned the gifts He would give to you. God knew what you would need and how it would benefit your life and the lives of others. His presents are personal and created by Him. When He gave the world His son, He took a risk because He knew that not every man would receive the gift. God gives us so much, freely without our even asking. Imagine if we were bold enough to ask of His unlimited resources.

Don't hesitate to ask Father God for more. If you are hesitant, then take that hesitation to Him and let Him transform your desire. Every good thing comes from Father God, and He enjoys giving.

Pray

Heavenly Father, forgive me when I hesitate to come to you. Thank you for your love and generosity. Help me to ask wisely and receive blessings so that I may bless others. In Jesus' name, amen.

Read and Confess

Read: James 4:2-3

Confess: I'm free to ask God everything in accordance with His Word.

Delve Deeper

Write about a time when you were friendly and welcoming. What did you do and how did you feel? Channel this experience when you need to be hospitable.

_____

_____

_____

_____

_____

Delve Deeper

How has money, work or social class affected your life?

Create
Create a master gift list.

Build a Habit
Congratulate and celebrate the success of others this week.

Put Faith into Action
Share a family recipe with a friend.

WEEK 17
SHARING YOUR LIGHT

Matthew 5:16

Let your light so shine before men, that they may see your good works and glorify your Father in heaven.

Sharing your light

Do you know the song "This Little Light of Mine"? As a child, I would sing loud and proud without concern of judgment from others. We should share our gifts in this manner. Yet somewhere along the way, we're told to quiet down, blend in. We need to trust the Holy Spirit. He will use our good works in ways that have the proper impact on others.

Your light is your talent, skill, or ability. It's the fire inside of you that you can't quench. Let it burn and blaze for the world to see. You have a God-given gift and a commandment to share your ability. Focus on glorifying Father God. You don't need to concern yourself with what others think. It's only about what Father God thinks. You need to share your talent with the world. It's the reason God created you and placed you where you are today. God put the light in you and put you on the hill. Trust the talent, vision, and ability that He gave.

Let your actions show that you're Christian. Use them to guide others to Christ by sharing your talents. The world sees Christ through His reflection in us. Walk in peace in the knowledge of your calling. Let your light shine to glorify God and know that you please Him.

Pray

Heavenly Father, Forgive me for times I want to hide the light you have given to me to share with the world. Thank you for the unquenchable fire set inside me. Help me to remember that I've been commanded to let it shine so that it brings glory to you. In Jesus' name, amen.

Read and Confess

Read: Proverbs 4:18

Confess: I let my light shine and it grows brighter and brighter over time because I walk in the path of the righteous.

Delve Deeper

When and how do you let your light shine?

_____
_____
_____
_____
_____
_____
_____

Delve Deeper
How can you be more generous with your talents?

_____

_____

_____

_____

Create

Create a list of encounters you can use to share God's love.

Build a Habit

Spend time outside each day and thank God for the light of the sun and the moon.

Put Faith into Action

Pray for those you work with and serve in your business.

WEEK 18
REJOICE

1 Thessalonians 5:16
Rejoice always...

Rejoice

Rejoicing can be like the Christian's opioid. Things may be falling apart around you, but you can still rejoice. You can take it all to God, and be thankful no matter what. Doing this allows the Christian to not become depressed or anxious by what may seem to be a disaster in the natural. The pain still exists, but your mind no longer comprehends it. This is the very peace of God that surpasses understanding.

If you have accepted Jesus Christ as your savior and know that you will go to heaven, you have reason to rejoice! No matter what happens in this realm, you can be joyful. If you struggle to rejoice, examine the trust you have in God. I know you believe that He exists, but you must be confident that He will use His power and forgiveness for you.

God is concerned with how we respond to life. Our response should be rejoicing, praying, and thanksgiving for everything. In the natural world, there may be a lot going on that is glum, distressing, and sad. Yet because we have Jesus, we can pray, give thanks and rejoice. Christ will provide the relief that we need to endure the troubles of this world.

Pray

Heavenly Father, please forgive me when I fail to rejoice always. Thank you for the gift of taking everything to you in prayer. Help me to obey your command to pray, rejoice and give thanks. In Jesus' name, amen.

Read and Confess

Read: John 16:33

Confess: I can rejoice because Christ has overcome the world.

Delve Deeper

What are your most amazing childhood memories and how can you create more opportunities to experience that type of joy today?

_____
_____
_____
_____
_____
_____
_____

Delve Deeper

What's the nicest thing anyone has done for you?

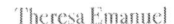

Create

Create a painting.

Build a Habit

This week eat without looking at your phone or television.

Put Faith into Action

Pray for someone you think has treated you unfairly.

PART TWO
MIND

WEEK 19
WORDS HAVE CREATIVE POWER

Genesis 1:3
Then God said, "Let there be light"; and there was light.

Words have creative power

Father God spoke the creation into existence. As His child, created in His image, be mindful of your words. They have creative power. They can bring both positive and negative into existence.

Christ is the creator. The book of John informs us that Christ created the world with God. Christ offers us His rest, relieving us from anxiety, stress, and fear. With this peace of mind, we can see that our work is good; just as Father God saw that His work was good. When we serve God, there's no need to distrust our actions.

Life and death are in the power of the tongue. Be mindful, be vigilant, but speak and create. Follow the example set by the Father. Speak via prayers, affirmations, and declarations. Declare your ideas and dreams to bring them to manifestation.

See it in your mind, believe it in your heart, and speak it into the universe. It is from the abundance of the heart that the mouth speaks. Without a belief in the heart, there is no creative power. We have the authority. Speak, and it will confirm what you endeavor in the earth realm. Heaven will stand in agreement with the child of God acting on the Word.

Pray

Dear Lord, forgive me when I speak negatively or doubt my gift. Thank you for creating me in your image with the ability to create. Remind me to always speak life to my creative ability. In Jesus' name, amen.

Read and Confess

Read: Proverbs 18:21
Confess: I speak life.

Delve Deeper

How are you speaking life to your divine dreams and desires?

_____
_____
_____
_____
_____
_____
_____
_____

Delve Deeper

In what ways do you see your work as good?

Create

Create encouraging sidewalk art.

Build a Habit

Refrain from complaining or speaking negativity this week.

Put Faith into Action

Call someone who's been on your mind lately. Share an encouraging word and offer to pray with them.

WEEK 20
TEND AND KEEP

Genesis 2:15
Then the Lord God took the man and put him in the garden of Eden to tend and keep it.

Tend and keep

The first man had a God-given purpose, and so do you. Father God gave us an assignment. We're here to tend and keep His creation. When we walk according to the purpose of His design, we walk in joy. It is a great responsibility, but it is also very freeing. Because God created the world, we don't have to worry about gaining anything or losing anything because it was never ours.

Father God taught Adam how to tend to the garden. Therefore He'll teach what you need to know as well. It is all a part of building a personal relationship with Him. God created man to be active. Our job is to do our part to protect, cherish, maintain, and look after the area of creation that God has entrusted to us.

Even before the fall of man, God created us to work, lovingly serve Him, and help Him fulfill a purpose. The work is part of creating a unique bond. God puts us in a specific place to do service for Him. The service we do is loving Him and caring for Him. We have God's nature of caring, so He fulfills that need by letting us care for Him. If we do this, we will have complete pleasure and joy.

Pray

Heavenly Father, forgive me when I become anxious about my assignment and don't focus on caring for you. Thank you for providing me with everything I need to be of service to you and work in partnership with you. Help me to keep my focus on my number one priority of loving you so that I can fulfill my responsibilities and experience joy. In Jesus' name, amen.

Read and Confess

Read: Ecclesiastes 9:7-10
Confess: I can enjoy life because God is pleased with me.

Delve Deeper

Of the tasks you performed today, which were most energizing and which were most draining?

_____

_____

_____

_____

_____

_____

Delve Deeper

What would make your physical workspace more efficient and more pleasant?

_____

_____

_____

_____

_____

Create

Create a greeting card collection so you're always ready to send words of comfort or congratulations.

Build a Habit

This week, take responsibility for your happiness rather than expecting someone else to make you happy.

Put Faith into Action

Donate to a local hospital.

WEEK 21
WORKING AS FOR GOD

Colossians 3:23
And whatever you do, do it heartily, as to the Lord and not to men...

Working as for God

There are many stories out there of people not doing their best, and it ends up hurting not only them in the end. I'm sure there have been times in your life when someone has made a simple remark or taken a simple action that profoundly affected you. The same is true in reverse. What you say and do has a profound effect on others. If we do everything as to the Lord, we can help ensure the impact we have will be positive.

One of my dental patients passed away from cancer, and his wife wrote me a beautiful note. It stated that he didn't like health care professionals, but he appreciated me. This news surprised me because I knew he was not a fan of the dentist. Yet it was a reminder of how much trust people put in me due to my title. It reminded me how much influence and responsibility comes with that trust.

As believers, we have a title and duty to uphold as well. When we do everything as to the Lord, we can be sure we always present our best work and the best impression for the Kingdom of God. The things we do and say matter. Our actions impact the lives of others. When we work for the Lord, we can work enthusiastically. We bring our best work when we have the attitude of working for the Lord.

Pray

Father in Heaven, forgive me when I am careless in work and words. Thank you for your Word and the reminder that it is the Lord I serve at all times. Help me to always do my best work in an enthusiastic manner so that I may uphold the trust placed in me as a believer. In Jesus' name, amen.

Confess

I enthusiastically do my best work at all times as though I serve the Lord and not man.

Delve Deeper

What inspires you?

_____

_____

_____

_____

_____

_____

_____
_____
_____
_____
_____
_____
_____
_____

Delve Deeper

What attributes do you have that make you feel grateful?

_____
_____
_____
_____
_____
_____
_____
_____
_____
_____

_____

_____

_____

_____

Create

Create a short story.

Build a Habit

Keep your physical or virtual desktop neat and clear this week.

Put Faith into Action

Encourage or mentor someone in your field of work.

WEEK 22
GROW UP

1 Peter 1:13

Therefore gird up the loins of your mind, be sober, and rest your hope fully upon the grace that is to be brought to you at the revelation of Jesus Christ ...

Grow up

Get prepared to push through any trouble and suffering you may experience along the way to fulfilling your dreams. You are building your mental capacity. Father God will use what you learn to make you the distinct person you need to be. So be a good steward of these blessings. Care for them as though they were God's because they are. Knowing that God is molding you should give you hope for the future.

Hope can be a sense of trust. We need to trust God to experience peace and confidence. Rely on God to help you fight through any fear. Get ready to share yourself. It may be scary at times, but you need to grow up and be obedient to the call God has made on your life. With the dream, God has given favor and blessings. Be dutiful to fulfill the obligations.

Take care of your responsibilities. You only have what you are well able to handle. God knows you and what you are capable of, more than you know yourself. Trust Him, and fulfill the plans He has given to you. There is a purpose for those dreams, and fulfilling them will bring glory to God.

Pray

Heavenly Father, please forgive my resistance to the challenges I face as I push toward my goals. Thank you for every obstacle along the way that makes me the person I need to be to serve you. Help me to keep your goal in mind every step of the way. In Jesus' name, amen.

Confess

I'm psyched up. I'm ready for a life shaped by God.

Delve Deeper

What gives you hope for the future?

_____

_____

_____

_____

_____

_____

_____

_____
_____
_____
_____
_____
_____

Delve Deeper

In what way are you mentally prepared to share your gift with the world?

_____
_____
_____
_____
_____
_____
_____
_____
_____
_____

_____

_____

_____

_____

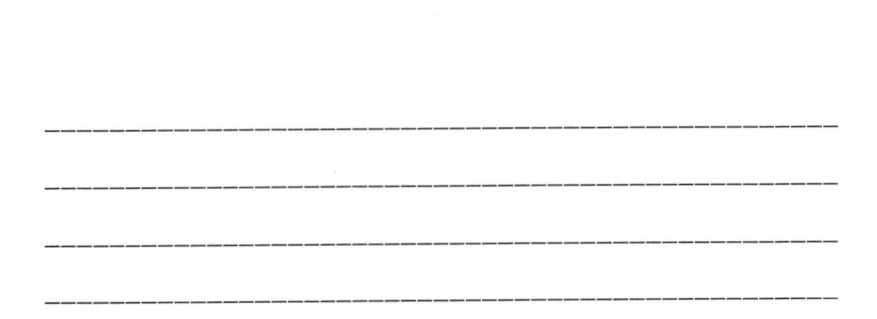

Create

Create a mind map of your hopes and dreams.

Build a habit

Each day this week, review the mind map you create. It will help you to stay focused on your hopes and dreams.

Put Faith into Action

Pray for the manifestation of one of your dreams. If you'd like to pray together, set up a call with me at calm.p31virtues.com.

WEEK 23
WEAPONS AGAINST FEAR

2 Timothy 1:7
For God has not given us a spirit of fear, but of power and of love and of a sound mind.

Weapons against fear

Created in the image of the creator makes us creative. Yet fear causes us to shrink back from our creative desires. We shrink back from the calling we hear from the Father. Depriving the world of what He placed us on earth to provide. The enemy assaults us by questioning; are you creative? Then he follows with endless what-ifs. What if you fail? What if you're not good enough? Will your creative venture pay the bills? What if you share yourself and people dismiss you? Take heart. Know that fear is a spirit of the enemy. We have the tools of power, love, and a sound mind to defeat the spirit of fear.

Power is our divine ability from the Holy Spirit. It is the power of God that allows us to create anything of worth. So take the pressure off of yourself and lean on the Lord. Create what pleases Him and trust Him to put your creativity to work. Work to please God and forget what man may say about you.

Love causes you to reach out rather than shrink back. It is love that allows us to be generous and vulnerable. Through love, we can make a connection that reaches the humanity of others. It is love that provides the transformative power of our creations.

The Word of God revives the mind. It protects mental processes and emotions. Let the Holy Spirit guide your thoughts rather than fear. Lean into the power, love, and self-control provided by the Father whenever the enemy makes you doubt your calling.

Pray

Father in Heaven, forgive me when I shrink back from my creative desires. Thank you for power, love and a sound mind. When I'm tempted to shrink back, help me to remember these fear-fighting gifts. In Jesus' name, amen.

Read and Confess

Read: Psalm 112:7
Confess: I trust in the Lord, I will not be afraid.

Delve Deeper

If you were the world's leading expert in your field, how would you behave?

_____

_____

_____

_____

_____

Cultivate Calm: The Weekly Devotional Study for Multifaceted Christian Women

_____
_____
_____
_____
_____
_____
_____
_____
_____
_____

Delve Deeper

What are some specific areas where you find yourself shrinking back rather than being vulnerable?

_____
_____
_____
_____
_____
_____
_____
_____

_____

_____

_____

_____

_____

_____

_____

Create

Start working on or finish a creative project God has put on your heart.

Build a Habit

Share your smile every time you enter a room.

Put Faith into Action

Share with the world a creative work that you've been holding onto.

WEEK 24
LACK OF KNOWLEDGE

Hosea 4:6

My people are destroyed for lack of knowledge. Because you have rejected knowledge, I also will reject you from being priest for Me; Because you have forgotten the law of your God, I also will forget your children.

Lack of knowledge

Empowerment is Supernatural, not Superficial. That is the tagline for my business. Worldly people want to erase God from the picture, yet take His spiritual laws to put to work in their lives. However, without true communion with God, a woman is defeated.

In the same way that gravity works for everyone regardless of whether they are a scientist or even believe in science, some spiritual laws operate the same for believers and non-believers alike. Yet, using spiritual laws in this way is a rejection of knowledge. It denies the power of the Word and the Holy Spirit. If you do not have a relationship with Father God, then you are utterly defeated. If you have knowledge of God but dismiss Him, it will result in shame. The grace of God is not permission to sin but a call to contend and overcome by abiding in Him.

Get the full benefits of being a believer. Read the Word and commune with the Holy Spirit. Gain knowledge and then enlightenment. Wisdom is using knowledge properly. It is the use of information or putting our faith into action that changes our lives. God should not be used as a cover. Make sure that the Word is in your heart. Be sure to study and tap into the full supernatural power of the Word.

Pray

Father God, forgive me when I seek the benefits of the Word without seeking a real relationship with you. Thank you for your Word, your grace and your mercy. Help me to grow in knowledge and wisdom so that I may enjoy the full supernatural power of the Word. In Jesus' name, amen.

Read and Confess

Read: Proverbs 10:23
Confess: I am mindful and enjoy wisdom.

Delve Deeper

How much do you know about Father God?

_____

_____

_____

_____

_____

Delve Deeper

What are some things you should do differently to improve your business?

Create
Create a reading list to enrich your mind.

Build a Habit
Read something from your reading list every day this week.

Put Faith into Action
Give help to someone who needs it.

WEEK 25
THE POWER TO SUCCEED

Deuteronomy 8:18
And you shall remember the Lord your God, for it is He who gives you power to get wealth, that He may establish His covenant which He swore to your fathers, as it is this day.

The power to succeed

You do nothing alone. It is all done through the Father. Earthly success comes from Father God to further His Kingdom. He provides the ideas. Then He supplies the stamina and emotional strength to execute the ideas. Your intelligence, drive, and diligence to succeed are blessings from God. When success comes, give thanks. Then value and savor it.

As women, we wear multiple hats in multiple arenas. We assume many roles, and we function differently in each of them. We must know how to best navigate in a variety of situations to achieve success. God gives us the power to be bold and the power to nurture. Rely on the Holy Spirit to provide the insight to know how to show up in each situation. Realize that there are situations that are beyond your control. You may need to put a message out just once. You may need to be involved in every detail. In all instances, allow the Holy Spirit to minister over the affair.

Use your gifts and innate nature as a woman to further the Kingdom of God. Allow the Holy Spirit to give you wisdom. Rely on this power to be successful in all aspects of life.

Pray

Heavenly Father, forgive me when I try to do things on my own. Thank you for the power to get wealth and succeed. Thank you for wisdom from the Holy Spirit. Help me to lean into the power from the Holy Spirit to succeed and further Your Kingdom. In Jesus' name, amen.

Read and Confess

Read: Psalm 18:32

Confess: God gives me strength and makes my way perfect.

Delve Deeper

Write about a time when you were powerful. What did you do and how did you feel? Channel this experience when you need to be powerful.

_____

_____

_____

_____

_____

_____

Delve Deeper

How do your actions demonstrate that you trust God with all of your thoughts and emotions?

_____
_____
_____
_____
_____

Create

Create a schedule that allows you to fulfill all your roles.

Build a Habit

Look people in the eye when you're speaking with them.

Put Faith into Action

Stand in your power and put out your message in the manner directed by the Holy Spirit.

WEEK 26
LIMITING BELIEFS

Romans 12:2
And do not be conformed to this world, but be transformed by the renewing of your mind, that you may prove what is that good and acceptable and perfect will of God.

Limiting beliefs

Let's talk about limiting beliefs. How many times have you heard something and accepted it as the truth? Those in this world or those outside of your field may be quick to say something is impossible. This world repeats negativity so much it can become accepted as truth. Do not allow this negativity to affect your mindset.

On a real estate coaching call, the coach expressed amazement by how a student continued to find amazing deals. The student stated that first, you have to believe that the opportunities exist, and then you go out and find them. When working with Realtors looking for investment properties, my husband and I often surprise them with the deals we can find. If you do not believe that something is possible, you will never look for it to happen or take the actions necessary to bring it to manifestation.

What you believe affects the steps you are willing to take. Limiting beliefs will affect your confessions and your ability to put the Word of God into action. Faith comes by hearing. Guard your hearing, study the Bible, and stay in tune with the Holy Spirit. You can blindly go along with the world, but God has a better way. Get clear on the goals that God has for your life. Take your thoughts and actions to give to God as a gift. Do not let this world limit your beliefs.

Pray

Father in Heaven, forgive me when I limit my beliefs to those of this world. Thank you for your Word and its mind renewing ability. Help me to bring my thoughts in line with the vision you have for my life so that I may take action and bring glory to you. In Jesus' name, amen.

Read and Confess

Read: Luke 1:37

Confess: With God, all things are possible.

Delve Deeper

What lies of the world do you believe?

_____

_____

_____

_____

_____

_____

Delve Deeper

Make a list of scriptures that refute the beliefs you listed above.

_____
_____
_____
_____
_____

Create

Create a strategy to live the life God has planned for you.

Build a Habit

If you find yourself having negative thoughts this week, give thanks to God for something you're grateful for in life.

Put Faith into Action

Declutter your home and your mind. Get rid of anything that isn't serving your ability to do God's will.

WEEK 27
YOUR ADVERSARY

1 Peter 5:8
Be sober, be vigilant; because your adversary the devil walks about like a roaring lion, seeking whom he may devour.

Your adversary

If you're going through a rough time, know that you're not alone. Know that what you're going through will not impact the plans God has for your life. Don't allow difficulties to cause you to open doors for the devil. Be strong in the faith by communing with God daily. Keep your passion in its proper place. Don't allow worries about your business, family, or life consume your mind and keep you from seeking the face of God.

The first time I took organic chemistry, I failed the course. One of my counselors suggested that maybe a career as a healthcare professional was not the right path for me. During the dental school application process, the failing grade was something I had to explain in my interviews. But God opened doors for me, and I even received a scholarship to attend dental school. The devil will seek and roar, but if you're watchful and faithful, he will not be able to come against you.

The enemy would not come against you if you were not a threat. The devil is seeking, but he needs permission to devour you. Sin opens the door to the devil. Protect your mind and your house. Don't be swayed in your commitment. If you have tried before and been unsuccessful, don't let the devil use it against you. Your past is not an indication of your future.

Pray

Father in Heaven, forgive me when I feel alone and allow the devil to hold my past over me. Thank you for the forgiveness of my sins and the plans you have for my future. Help me as I continue to work towards that future so that I may bring you glory. In Jesus' name, amen.

Delve Deeper

Where do you see yourself five years from now? What can you do now to improve life in the present?

_____

_____

_____

_____

_____

_____

_____

_____

Delve Deeper

How can you expand your mind so that you see yourself the way God sees you?

_____
_____
_____
_____

Create

Create some variety in your normal routine. Try something new or drive a different route.

Build a Habit

Stand tall; focus on good posture this week.

Put Faith into Action

Hold your tongue and don't speak negatively or needlessly.

WEEK 28
EXCELLENCE

Proverbs 22:29
**Do you see a man who excels in his work?
He will stand before kings;
He will not stand before unknown men.**

Excellence

Excellent people want to hire the best, be part of the best, and nurture the best. When I was shopping for a cake vendor for my wedding, I selected the pastry chef who reminded me of myself. He was someone very particular about his work. I knew I would receive the best and would be more than satisfied with the outcome.

When you see the product of someone who takes pride in their work, it speaks to you on a multitude of levels. It makes you eager and willing to employ their services because you know the high standard to which they hold themselves. Working with the best people makes you want to up your game. You raise your standards to be comparable to them. When you see yourself in someone younger, it makes you want to reach out and encourage them. You seize the opportunity to serve or minister to another. You push them to pursue and achieve their goals.

When you know you are worthy, you will not settle. You will stay faithful and fixed in your commitment to doing the will of God. Those who are sloppy in their lives will not want to be around you. Excellence creates boundaries helping you surround yourself with like-minded Christians.

Pray

Dear Lord, forgive me when I get sloppy in my work and life. Thank you for the example of Christ to live an exemplary life. Help me to stay fixed and focused on that example so that I may accomplish my purpose in a manner that is pleasing to you. In Jesus' name, amen.

Read and Confess

Read: Proverbs 1:5
Confess: I listen and learn from those who are wise.

Delve Deeper

How would the 3-5-sentence summary of your life read?

_____
_____
_____
_____
_____
_____
_____

Delve Deeper

What inspires you to excellence?

_____
_____
_____
_____

Create

Create boundaries in your life to weed out those who detract from your excellence.

Build a Habit

This week, be willing to say no if something isn't for you.

Put Faith into Action

Perform your work with excellence this week.

WEEK 29
TITHING

Malachi 3:8-10

"Will a man rob God?
Yet you have robbed Me!
But you say,
'In what way have we robbed You?'
In tithes and offerings.
[9] You are cursed with a curse,
For you have robbed Me,
Even this whole nation.
[10] Bring all the tithes into the storehouse,
That there may be food in My house,
And try Me now in this,"
Says the Lord of hosts,
"If I will not open for you the windows of heaven
And pour out for you such blessing
That there will not be room enough to receive it.

Tithing

This verse is powerful to me because it is a reminder that I'm a steward, and obedience has a great reward. I think anyone who tithes will tell you the benefits. Unfortunately, I don't believe that testimony is necessarily beneficial in this area. Even if someone tells you they tithe, you may not see the benefits they're experiencing because people tend to be private about their finances. But faith is not the substance of things you can see, and tithing is very much an act of faith.

I'm just like you and not always rational when it comes to money and finances. I believe God supplies all my need according to His infinite riches. I believe everything I have belongs to God, and I am merely a steward of that which He has entrusted me. I once only dreamt of making the financial achievements I see God work in my life.

It took me many years to let go of the fear and start tithing. When I did decide to begin tithing, I had nothing to lose because I was unemployed with nothing but a degree and debt. The best advice I can give you if you want to tithe but aren't there yet is to pray. Tell God everything you're feeling in this area and know that God keeps His word.

Pray

Dear Father, forgive my fear when it comes to tithing. Thank you for your challenge in this area. Help me to take you up on that challenge so that I may experience all that you have to offer for my life to the benefit of your kingdom. In Jesus' name, amen.

Read and Confess

Read: 2 Corinthians 9:6-7

Confess: I give generously and delightfully to the Kingdom of God.

Delve Deeper

What prevents you from being more generous with your finances?

_____
_____
_____
_____
_____
_____
_____
_____
_____
_____
_____
_____
_____
_____
_____
_____
_____

Delve Deeper

Write a testimony of God's faithfulness in your life over the past week.

_____
_____
_____
_____
_____
_____
_____
_____
_____
_____
_____
_____
_____
_____
_____

Create

Create a card and a small gift bag for your delivery people.

Build a Habit

This week carry cash and give it away.

Put Faith into Action

Start tithing or give beyond your tithe this week.

WEEK 30
WALK IN THE PATH CREATED

Ephesians 2:10
For we are His workmanship, created in Christ Jesus for good works, which God prepared beforehand that we should walk in them.

Walk in the path created

Walk in the path that Father God created for you. When a door opens, you have to walk through it because it may soon close. We don't have to open the doors; we only have to walk through them. We don't have to plow down the trees because God provides the path. Walk.

Enjoy a sense of ease in life by walking in the path created. Make the Word a part of your mindset so that you can have the faith needed to trust all the benefits and blessings God has for you. Trust God to open the doors for you to walk through. If God has put something on your heart, even though no one among your family, friends, or acquaintances has accomplished it, do not let it become a limitation for you. When I made a career change by leaving the Air Force, I hesitated to go to dental school right away. A door opened by way of a phone call providing a scholarship for me to attend my first-choice school. I walked through the door, receiving the blessing along with the opportunity of blessing others.

Don't limit God with your limiting beliefs. Don't allow what others say or what others experience to override the opportunities that God is laying before you. God may have a plan for your life that differs from them. Trust Him.

Pray

Father in Heaven, please forgive me for my hesitation to walk on the path that you provide. Forgive my limiting beliefs. Thank you for the doors you open for me, strengthen my mindset so that I'm obedient in walking through them to bring you glory. In Jesus' name, amen.

Confess

I walk in the path God has created for me, free from any curses of my ancestors.

Delve Deeper

What are some negative things you think about your life? Are they true?

_____

_____

_____

_____

_____

_____
_____
_____
_____
_____
_____
_____
_____
_____
_____

Delve Deeper

What risks that you need to take to move forward in life?

_____
_____
_____
_____
_____
_____
_____
_____
_____

_____
_____
_____
_____
_____
_____
_____

Create

Create a self-guided walking tour of your city.

Build a Habit

Ask yourself better questions this week. Ask "How" rather than "Can."

Put Faith into Action

Refrain from judging others this week.

WEEK 31
FILLED WITH CREATIVITIY

Exodus 35:35
He has filled them with skill to do all manner of work of the engraver and the designer and the tapestry maker, in blue, purple, and scarlet thread, and fine linen, and of the weaver—those who do every work and those who design artistic works.

Filled with creativity

You have been given your skill and talent from your creator. Father God created the heavens and the earth and you. You are creative because you are His image. Don't doubt your skills and ability. Lean into your God-given talent.

I'm passionate about dentistry. I was treating a young patient in the dental office and he asked me, with disdain, "Why would you want to be a dentist anyway?" Laughing, I replied that everyone is different. For me, dentistry is the perfect mix of science and art. Most of the time, I receive immediate gratification for my efforts. I also enjoy the variety of tasks and the people that I meet during the day.

God has filled me with the skill, the grace, and the joy to do the work that I do. When there is a doubt on my part, I ask for help. I pray for the blessing of my hands, my eyes, and mouth to detect, diagnose, treat disease, and communicate with my patients.

Be thankful for the creative gift that Father God has given to you. Let it bring you joy and empowerment. Ask God for help to improve your talent. Then, use your creative ability to be a blessing to others.

Pray

Heavenly Father, I am delighted to be created in your image and I'm thankful for my creative abilities. I'm sorry for the times that I fail to use my creativity to bless others. Please help me to strengthen my talents and use them for your glory. In Jesus' name, amen.

Confess

I am gifted by the grace of God.

Delve Deeper

What creative activities cause me to lose track of time?

_____

_____

_____

_____

_____

_____

_____

_____

Delve Deeper

What role does my creativity play in making differences in the lives of others?

_____
_____
_____

Create

Create a swipe file to store the great ideas and inspiration you get from others.

Build a Habit

Be willing to take risks this week.

Put Faith into Action

Make friends with those who share your beliefs and creative passions.

WEEK 32
GOD IS FAITHFUL

1 Corinthians 10:13

No temptation has overtaken you except such as is common to man; but God is faithful, who will not allow you to be tempted beyond what you are able, but with the temptation will also make the way of escape, that you may be able to bear it.

God is faithful

Even though you are a multifaceted Christian woman, you will not be overburdened. Never question your ability to get it all done. You may have lots of titles and roles to fulfill and an endless to-do list. You may have lots of people counting on you for help and survival. It may seem overwhelming and impossible to get everything done. But God is faithful.

You are not alone. You are not the only person on the planet who is going through the challenges you are facing. These are everyday challenges. Women have dealt with these issues since the fall of man. Father God promises that you will be able to bear all that you have to handle. Your limit exceeds your current challenge. God tests you because He knows that you are ready for the test and that you will not only pass but will excel. If He did not prove you, you would never know all that you are capable of achieving as you abide in Him.

Have faith in the Father who trusts you with all the roles He has assigned to you. Be encouraged by those who have gone before you. Look at and consult with the faithful women in your circle for encouragement. God knows you are well able to excel. Push through and see for yourself what God already knows.

Pray

Heavenly Father, please forgive me when I feel overwhelmed. Thank you for your promise to be faithful and not allow me to be tested beyond my limit. Help me to rise to the challenges before me with confidence in my ability to pass the test because I abide in you. In Jesus' name, amen.

Read and Confess

Read: 2 Timothy 2:13
Confess: God remains faithful even when I struggle.

Delve Deeper

How do you relax when you're feeling stressed?

_____

_____

_____

_____

_____

Delve Deeper

How can you improve the quality of the time spent with loved ones?

Create

Create a walking group with your friends or neighbors.

Build a Habit

Participate in a weekly prayer call.

Put Faith into Action

Follow up with encouragement when someone tells you about an upcoming event such as a doctor's visit, job interview or test.

WEEK 33
DON'T QUIT

Galatians 6:9

And let us not grow weary while doing good, for in due season we shall reap if we do not lose heart.

Don't quit

At a real estate investing seminar, my husband received the book *Total Money Makeover* by Dave Ramsey. We liked the idea of living debt-free and decided to implement the baby steps described in the book. We had every type of debt at the time, including student loans, car loans, credit card debt, and home mortgages. In the beginning, it was exciting to pay down a bill and roll the money into the next debt. However, by the time we got to the home mortgages, we felt as though we were no longer making progress.

It was extremely slow, and we were wondering if debt freedom would happen for us or if it was worth the effort. Thanks to God, we came across this scripture. It was confirmation that we were doing the right thing and that we needed to continue.

In this day and age, we're used to rapid results. Yet, sometimes there are multiple steps required to achieve a goal. During these times, it is necessary to stay motivated and focused to avoid giving up just short of winning the prize.

Pray

Heavenly Father, Forgive me when I want to give up short of the goal line. Thank you for the truth of your Word. Help me to maintain the passion I begin with all the way through to the end. In Jesus' name, amen.

Confess

I receive my reward because I maintain my passion.

Delve Deeper

What does it mean to do good?

_____
_____
_____
_____
_____
_____
_____
_____
_____
_____

Delve Deeper

What can you do to renew your passion in an area where you are currently struggling?

Create
Create a photo album from a photography walk.
Build a Habit
Ask open-ended questions this week.
Put Faith into Action
Engage in a random act of kindness.

WEEK 34
BOLD THOUGHT AND ACTIONS

2 Corinthians 10:3-5

For though we walk in the flesh, we do not war according to the flesh. [4] **For the weapons of our warfare are not carnal but mighty in God for pulling down strongholds,** [5] **casting down arguments and every high thing that exalts itself against the knowledge of God, bringing every thought into captivity to the obedience of Christ...**

Bold thoughts and actions

We have to be bold in the world to do things that are contrary to popular opinion. We have to resist the bombardment of media that markets a life that is opposed to the will of God. We must be on guard to recognize things that are against God and cast them out accordingly. So much truth of the Bible is presented but without crediting the author; these partial truths can be seductive and get us into trouble.

We need to know the whole truth and act accordingly. If we want to be bold in our actions, we have to be daring in our thoughts. As believers, our minds can bring together our body and spirit to live as God originally intended. We must be sure our thinking is of the beliefs of a child of God because our thoughts affect our emotions. Before every response, there is a thought. The world tries to convince us that we should "feel" happy and that we should take actions based on our emotions, but feelings are unreliable.

Christ should be our only delight. The world can manipulate us into thinking that joy should come from approval or shiny objects. The world would have us put someone or something else in place of Christ in our lives. God gives us every gift, and Christ should captivate us. The power to bring our thoughts into captivity allows us to rise above our emotions and live life delighted in Christ. This boldness is the genius power of our thoughts.

Pray

Dear Father in Heaven, forgive me when I let my feelings allow me to be seduced by the world. Thank you for the ability to bring my thoughts into captivity so that I may delight in Christ only and live a life of obedience. In Jesus' name, amen.

Confess

I think and act according to the Word and not according to my feelings.

Delve Deeper

How would you spend your time if you had all the money in the world?

_____

_____

_____
_____
_____
_____
_____
_____
_____
_____
_____
_____
_____
_____
_____

Delve Deeper

How does music influence you?

_____
_____
_____
_____
_____
_____

_____

_____

_____

_____

_____

_____

_____

_____

_____

Create

Create a mail sorting station.

Build a Habit

This week, be completely honest with yourself.

Put Faith into Action

Be willing to be inconvenienced this week.

WEEK 35
PERSONAL EXPERIENCE

Matthew 14:13-21

When Jesus heard it, He departed from there by boat to a deserted place by Himself. But when the multitudes heard it, they followed Him on foot from the cities. [14] And when Jesus went out He saw a great multitude; and He was moved with compassion for them, and healed their sick. [15] When it was evening, His disciples came to Him, saying, "This is a deserted place, and the hour is already late. Send the multitudes away, that they may go into the villages and buy themselves food." [16] But Jesus said to them, "They do not need to go away. You give them something to eat." [17] And they said to Him, "We have here only five loaves and two fish." [18] He said, "Bring them here to Me." [19] Then He commanded the multitudes to sit down on the grass. And He took the five loaves and the two fish, and looking up to heaven, He blessed and broke and gave the loaves to the disciples; and the disciples gave to the multitudes. [20] So they all ate and were filled, and they took up twelve baskets full of the fragments that

remained. [21] Now those who had eaten were about five thousand men, besides women and children.

Personal experience

At the feeding of the five thousand, the disciples experienced the satisfaction of a meal. Then they received, on top of that, a basket of leftover broken pieces. Christ gave thanks and broke the loaves before giving them to the people. Broken is considered a bad thing, damaged. Yet, in this instance, it was a necessity. From the broken loaves, everyone ate to satisfaction.

After eating, the disciples picked up twelve baskets. That means that each disciple had the opportunity to personally experience the gift of God's abundance. As we walk out in faith doing what God has called us to, we encounter the benefits, and as a result, our faith grows. We continue to take steps and experience the abundance of life in Christ. We walk by faith, but when that faith becomes manifest, we perceive it with our physical senses.

Today we use the term "broken" for having given up all hope. Broken is equivalent to despair. However, Christ gave those broken pieces to give hope, and as a demonstration of God's ability to exceed above anything we can imagine. We go through a lot of personal experiences in this realm. Some of those experiences leave us broken, yet this scripture shows that abundance and satisfaction are within the brokenness.

Pray

Heavenly Father, forgive me for my despair and the lack of faith that accompanies it. Thank you for your ability to do above anything I can imagine. Help me to embrace the experiences I have in this realm knowing that the outcome will be abundance and satisfaction. In Jesus' name, amen.

Read and Confess

Read: Ecclesiastes 3:13

Confess: I enjoy the satisfaction and abundance of my personal experiences.

Delve Deeper

What experience would you like to have again, for the first time?

Delve Deeper

What have you learned from people of other generations?

_____
_____
_____
_____
_____
_____
_____
_____
_____
_____
_____
_____
_____
_____

Create

Create kits for an animal or homeless shelter.

Build a Habit

Batch your errands and tasks to maximize your time.

Put Faith into Action
Give an experience gift to someone.

WEEK 36
SIMPLIFY

Romans 8:5-6

For those who live according to the flesh set their minds on the things of the flesh, but those who live according to the Spirit, the things of the Spirit. ⁶ For to be carnally minded is death, but to be spiritually minded is life and peace.

Simplify

Let's simplify. There are so many things to be done as a multifaceted woman. We have so many earthly things to accomplish. However, we must remember to live according to the Spirit of God. Then, we will realize there is just one thing: love.

Christ came for one purpose. He did other things while He walked the earth, but He always kept His mission clear. God calls us to love Him and to love our neighbor. All that we do should fall under the heading of love. When we serve in the role of daughter, wife, or mother, we do so with love. When we function as employees, creators, founders, CEOs, or thought leaders, we operate with love.

Therefore we can take the pressure off ourselves and understand that if we are working with devotion, we are fulfilling our assignment.

Take your mind off yourself and put your mind on Father God. Take your mind off this world, and focus on the Kingdom of God. Let Father God tend to your flesh. He knows what you need. Spend your time managing your calling of love. When you focus on this, all else will work itself out. You will be able to go forth from a place of peace.

Pray

Dear Lord, I'm sorry for spending so much time focusing on myself and my to do list. Please forgive me. Thank you for giving me the ability to simplify by focusing on you and sharing your love with the world. In Jesus' name, amen.

Confess

Jesus loves me.

Delve Deeper

What mindset shifts would increase your peace?

_____

_____

_____

_____

_____

_____

_____

_____

Delve Deeper

What mistakes are you making with your time?

_____

_____

Create

Create a capsule wardrobe or daily uniform.

Build a Habit

Only single-task this week.

Put Faith into Action

This week, monitor your thoughts. Replace any thoughts of worry by reciting the Word of God.

PART THREE
BODY

WEEK 37
YOUR BODY IS HOLY

1 Corinthians 3:16-17

Do you not know that you are the temple of God and that the Spirit of God dwells in you? [17] If anyone defiles the temple of God, God will destroy him. For the temple of God is holy, which temple you are.

Your body is holy

Be more holy. Be more dedicated to the will of God by caring for His temple. Have the willpower required for disciplined upkeep and diligent restraint. Doing so will increase your resolve and make your entire being better.

Care for your physical body. Protect the God-given systems created to keep your body in working order. Take care of your skin and immune system. Create habits that allow you to give your body the food, sleep, and exercise needed for peak performance. Healthy habits and routines will make your upkeep easier. Don't misuse or exploit your body. Remember, you will have to give account for your actions. This knowledge should improve your determination. Work to keep your body in its original state.

Have a lifestyle that allows self-care. Include simple indulgences that increase comfort and happiness. These self-care efforts will improve your mental health. Then you will be more equipped to reach out to care for others. You cannot be of service to others without caring for yourself.

Caring for the temple of God means that you will keep your body and mind healthy. You will maintain and protect your body. Profit your body so that you can benefit the kingdom of God.

Pray

Father in Heaven, forgive me for my neglect and abuse of your temple. Thank you for the amazing creation of my body in which you dwell. Keep me mindful that my body is holy so that I stay disciplined and diligent in maintaining it. In Jesus' name, amen.

Read and Confess

Read: Ephesians 5:29
Confess: I nourish and cherish my body.

Delve Deeper

How will you care for yourself differently knowing you are the temple of God? What will you do more of? What will you do less of?

_____

_____

_____

_____

Delve Deeper

What habits do you need to create so that willpower is no longer required to care for your body?

_____
_____
_____
_____
_____
_____
_____
_____

Create

Create a skincare routine.

Build a Habit

Only eat whole foods this week. Nothing processed or from a can or box.

Put Faith into Action

Arise each morning and thank God for your body. Promise Him to care for it today.

WEEK 38
PHYSICAL SENSES

Proverbs 15:30

The light of the eyes rejoices the heart, And a good report makes the bones healthy.

Physical senses

Our senses keep us safe. Healthy disciplines concerning our body influence every aspect of our tripartite being. Our eyes affect how we see and how we perceive. Our ears receive messages that can affect our entire being. Use your eyes and ears to maintain your purpose. Be sure your eyes and ears protect your heart.

The light we see with our eyes illuminates. We hear with our ears, and that hearing influences us. Both affect where we focus our attention. Eyes direct and show where to go. Our eyes prevent stumbling. Our ears hear suggestions and lessons that guide our actions. Without focused seeing and hearing, we're at risk. We can go off course from the direction of our divine purpose.

Good news we receive by seeing and hearing provides

nourishment. It helps feed and build the core of our being, the marrow of our bones, and the creation site for blood cells. Then the heart circulates the blood to the rest of the body. A person with good news has bright eyes. When you see their eyes light up, it makes you happy. Welcoming positive news is essential for good health. Read aloud and remind yourself of the good news of salvation. With that salvation comes physical health and healing by the stripes of Christ.

Pray

Heavenly Father, forgive me for not protecting my eyes and ears from negative influences. Thank you for my senses that keep me safe. Help me to use them in ways that keep both my body and spirit healthy. In Jesus' name, amen.

Read and Confess

Read: Isaiah 53:5
Confess: I am healed by the stripes of Christ.

Delve Deeper

Write three things you see right now for which you're grateful.

_____
_____
_____
_____
_____
_____
_____

_____
_____
_____
_____
_____
_____
_____

Delve Deeper

How are you protecting your eyes and ears from negative influences?

_____
_____
_____
_____
_____
_____
_____
_____
_____
_____
_____

_____
_____
_____
_____

Create

Create infused water in a clear container so you can see its beauty as you hydrate.

Build a Habit

Limit the news you watch, read and hear this week.

Put Faith into Action

Pray for the healing of someone on your church's prayer list.

WEEK 39
FELLOWSHIP

Acts 2:46-47

So continuing daily with one accord in the temple, and breaking bread from house to house, they ate their food with gladness and simplicity of heart, praising God and having favor with all the people. And the Lord added to the church daily those who were being saved.

Fellowship

We are the hands of God. One of the best ways to use our hands, invite others to the faith, and encourage those in the church is to dine together. God created us with a need for fellowship and hospitality. We need relationships in our lives. Sharing our homes and meals with others is a way to show the love of God.

Food is universal, so sharing a meal can be a simple way to bring people together. Food makes it safe for everyone to participate. Preparing the food, setting the table, passing the food, and cleaning up afterward can be done in cooperation with one another. Jobs done collectively are done with ease. The food provides a centerpiece and neutral topic of conversation. People feel happy and relaxed when they eat, and the food makes them feel welcome. Sitting at a table for a meal causes us to slow down to enjoy one another along with the food.

Relationships deepen, and those in attendance feel gladness when we slow down and savor our food. The fellowship makes us stronger because it helps us become united through prayer and belief. When we come together, we learn of other opportunities to serve our neighbors. Sharing ideas, recognizing that others go through the same things that you go through deepens human experiences and creates emotional connectivity. We know we're not alone because we share and grow together in faith. With hospitality, we can come together as a community and feel the presence of the Lord among us.

Pray

Heavenly Father, please forgive me when I fail to use my hands to offer hospitality to others. Thank you for the unifying gift of food to ease the way for deepened relationships through fellowship and hospitality. Help me to eagerly share that gift every time the opportunity presents itself. In Jesus' name, amen.

Confess

I use my hands to offer fellowship and hospitality.

Delve Deeper

What are some things others have said or done for you that made you feel cherished?

_____

_____

_____

Delve Deeper
What about your body makes you joyful?

_____
_____
_____
_____
_____
_____
_____

Create

Create a tidy up routine to use in preparation for last minute company.

Build a Habit

Be well groomed by planning your hair appointments, manicures and pedicures in advance.

Put Faith into Action

Share your blessings this week.

WEEK 40
FEAR AND HEALTH

Proverbs 3:5-8

Trust in the Lord with all your heart, And lean not on your own understanding; ⁶ In all your ways acknowledge Him, And He shall direct your paths. ⁷ Do not be wise in your own eyes; Fear the Lord and depart from evil. ⁸ It will be health to your flesh, And strength to your bones.

Fear and health

Healthy Christians bring glory to God. Life began in the spiritual realm and then came to the physical realm. Therefore, it's no wonder that fear of the Lord is the secret of health. God has instructed us to trust and abide in Him. You can rely on your understanding and experience stress, or trust the Lord and experience health.

Nourishment is food or the materials needed for growth, health, and wellness. Consuming the Word benefits both the spirit and the body. Rely on God's Word to provide nourishment for your body. He will give you what you need to live, grow, and be healthy.

Stress, on the other hand, is your reaction to fear, and it causes disease. It affects your immune system and your hormones. It affects your sleep. Major illnesses such as obesity, Alzheimer's, diabetes, and heart disease can occur due to stress and lack of sleep. Allowing your mind to get the best of you as you try to figure things out only leads to stress. Trust the Lord to give you guidance in every situation.

Your perceptions become reflected in your body. Healthy, positive thoughts lead to positive emotions. Those emotions release chemicals that lead to better health. Continue to feed on the Word, experience good health, and bring glory to God.

Pray

Dear Lord, forgive me when I try to figure things out on my own only to get stressed and frustrated. Thanks for your voice and Word to guide me. Help me remember to run to you for nourishment and answers. In Jesus' name, amen.

Read and Confess

Read: Isaiah 41:10

Confess: I will not panic because God is with me. God gives me strength and holds me steady.

Delve Deeper

How can you give God total access to your life so that He is acknowledged in everything you do?

_____

_____

_____

_____

Delve Deeper
What can you do to be attuned to God's voice everywhere you go?

_____
_____
_____
_____
_____
_____
_____

Create

Create an exercise routine. Exercise is proven to produce hormones that make us feel good, which improves our mood, reduces fear, and enhances overall health.

Build a Habit

Eat the rainbow this week to build and maintain your immune system.

Put Faith into Action

Pray to God about your health. Listen and act on the answer you receive.

WEEK 41
CHRIST MAGNIFIED IN YOUR BODY

Philippians 1:20

According to my earnest expectation and hope that in nothing I shall be ashamed, but with all boldness, as always, so now also Christ will be magnified in my body, whether by life or by death.

Christ magnified in your body

Trust God for the stamina to accomplish all the duties in your busy life. Magnify Christ in your body and your life. Let your mortality work for you. Chase the clock to get your life's work accomplished before the buzzer sounds. Awareness of your mortality can help you manifest.

You are only in this realm for a moment. While you are here, trust God with your natural body. You have the physical strength to rise to the call He has on your life. The day will not require more energy than you will have to give. Give all your energy and vitality to fulfill the dream God has given you. When you do everything for the Lord, you can't lose. Don't worry about your body. Yet care for it, as it is the temple of God. Operate as a steward, giving your whole to accomplish His commands. Aggressively put yourself out on the field of play. Don't save anything in reserve.

Live for today. Trust God to supply everything you need when you need it. Get your daily bread daily. You have plenty for today without the need to hoard for tomorrow. You've won. God will not leave you.

Pray

Heavenly Father, forgive me for holding back and not trusting you to provide the energy I need in my busy life. Thank you for every blessing and role you have given to me. Help me to remember that it is you that I serve and you who are magnified by my actions. In Jesus' name, amen.

Read and Confess

Read: Philippians 4:13

Confess: I can do all things through Christ who strengthens me.

Delve Deeper

How can you magnify Christ in your body?

_____

_____

_____

_____

_____

_____

_____

_____

Delve Deeper
What can you let go of to gain more energy?

_____
_____
_____

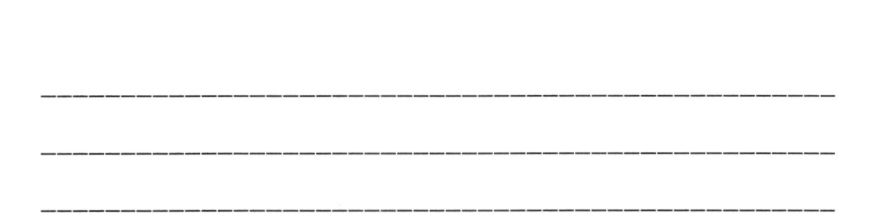

Create

Create a healthy meal plan to nourish your health and body.

Build a Habit

Start strength training.

Put Faith into Action

Repeat your confession and accomplish the items on your to do list.

WEEK 42
PEACE AND HEALING

Jeremiah 33:6
Behold, I will bring it health and healing; I will heal them and reveal to them the abundance of peace and truth.

Peace and healing

God offers peace and healing but are you receiving it? Invite peace into your life via self-care. Learn to experience all the benefits of living by the Word of God.

Early in my dental career, I was taught that to master pediatric dentistry I should possess calm throughout my entire being if I wanted my patient to be relaxed. It's impossible to give to others something that you don't have. Use self-care as your superpower to receive an overflowing cup to pour out onto others. Triage your body and life to target things that are giving you uneasiness. Be sure your cup is full before you take on duties or attempt to help another human being. It may be as simple as taking a drink of water before starting a project. There may be jobs that you could delegate or outsource. Identify the tasks that only you can do and focus on those responsibilities first.

Take your hopes and concerns to God at the start of the day and throughout the day. Thank God in advance for the results and peace along the way. Receive God's peace and feel ease throughout your entire body. The effects will be health, harmony, and blessings.

Pray

Dear Father in Heaven, forgive me for going along, ignoring the offer of peace and healing that you have for me. I am thankful that I can go to you at any time to have my cup refilled. Help me to maximize that benefit so that I can be a better blessing to others. In Jesus' name, amen.

Confess

I have health, healing and peace.

Delve Deeper

What thoughts and actions do you need to let go of to improve your health?

_____

_____

_____

_____

_____

_____

_____

Delve Deeper
How can you nurture your body in your alone time?

_____

_____

_____

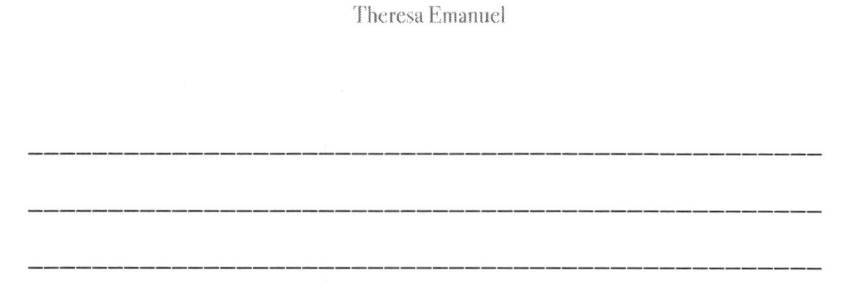

Create

Create a health care schedule for your annual physical, vision, dental and other health maintenance visits.

Build a Habit

Do balance promoting exercises this week.

Put Faith into Action

Invite someone to a homemade dinner.

WEEK 43
WHAT TO EAT

Genesis 1:29

And God said, "See, I have given you every herb that yields seed which is on the face of all the earth, and every tree whose fruit yields seed; to you it shall be for food.

What to eat

Father God gives us everything we need for success in life, including the food to nourish our bodies. He gives us everything. Think of this verse as the beginning of Him supplying all our needs according to His riches. It is all a gift given to us to steward on His behalf.

Today much of what we consume is causing disease. Due to manufacturing, the so-called food we gravitate to is hard to recognize as something Father God created. We get lazy and grab things we perceive as quick. When tempted to go this route, remember God's gift and your duty to steward. All that He gives us is for our benefit. We are obligated to make use of it and get a return.

God gives us food for life, increase, and well-being. The diet described in this verse is one that builds the immune system to protect us from attack. Vegetables and herbs have the nutrients and protein we need for the building blocks of our bodies. These nutrients help repair our cells. We should eat the food God first gave to us in a form most closely to the way He created it. Eat live food, raw and uncooked in its natural state. Then consume it in appropriate amounts for wellness. Eat the food God provided and experience good health.

Pray

Dear Lord, forgive me when I seek man-made processed food rather than the food you created for me to eat. Thank you for providing beautiful healthy food to nourish my body. Help me to make the right food choices through the prompting of the Holy Spirit. In Jesus' name, amen.

Confess

I am free from food addictions and eat food that keeps my body healthy.

Delve Deeper

Why do you eat? What are times that you choose less than healthy food choices? What need, other than hunger are you trying to fulfill?

_____

_____

_____

_____

_____

Cultivate Calm: The Weekly Devotional Study for Multifaceted Christian Women

_____
_____
_____
_____
_____
_____
_____
_____
_____
_____

Delve Deeper

How can you better recognize whether your hunger is physical or emotional?

_____
_____
_____
_____
_____
_____
_____
_____

_____
_____
_____
_____
_____
_____
_____

Create
Create an indoor herb garden.

Build a Habit
Plan for healthy meals out by looking at the menu in advance.

Put Faith into Action
Pray over your food as you prepare it and before you eat.

WEEK 44
BODY IMAGE

Psalm 139:13-14

For You formed my inward parts;
You covered me in my mother's womb.
[14] I will praise You, for I am fearfully and wonderfully made;
Marvelous are Your works,
And that my soul knows very well.

Body image

Praise God for the body He created for us. Let's be thankful for our bodies rather than critical of them. Let's appreciate all that our bodies can do for us and all that we can do with our body. As Christians, we should be mindful of what we see, hear, and confess.

Our souls know our worth as children handmade by God. Let's not expose ourselves to media that pushes unrealistic body images or objectives of the female body. Let's be aware of the contradictions in our society that affect our body and our body image. With this knowledge, we can avoid ups and downs in our self-worth. Let's be aware of our thoughts about our bodies and everything that affects our bodies. Let's control our thoughts about food, water, sleep, exercise, and fresh air.

Our thoughts, self-talk, self-care, and body image all come from the heart. How we treat and fuel our bodies is a reflection of what is in our heart regarding our body. Let's be good stewards of our bodies because of the love of God. When we are in a relationship with the creator, we never need to feel shame about our bodies. Radiance comes from being in contact with the creator.

Pray

Heavenly Father, forgive me when I think too lowly or too highly about my physical appearance. Thank you for the attention, care and love you put into creating me. Help me to look to you as I steward my body so I know that it's you that produces radiance. In Jesus' name, amen.

Read and Confess

Read: Song of Solomon 7:6
Confess: My beauty within and without is absolute.

Delve Deeper

Is your struggle with body image really idolatry? Do you think that beautiful people have more fulfilling lives?

_____
_____
_____
_____
_____

Delve Deeper

If you knew your body would never change in appearance from how it looks today, would you eat, exercise or dress differently?

Create

Create a home spa to nurture your body.

Build a Habit

Floss every day this week.

Put Faith into Action

Pray that you will be able to see yourself as God sees you.

WEEK 45
FAITH AND YOUR BODY

Luke 8:43-48

Now a woman, having a flow of blood for twelve years, who had spent all her livelihood on physicians and could not be healed by any, [44] came from behind and touched the border of His garment. And immediately her flow of blood stopped. [45] And Jesus said, "Who touched Me?" When all denied it, Peter and those with him said, "Master, the multitudes throng and press You, and You say, 'Who touched Me?'" [46] But Jesus said, "Somebody touched Me, for I perceived power going out from Me." [47] Now when the woman saw that she was not hidden, she came trembling; and falling down before Him, she declared to Him in the presence of all the people the reason she had touched Him and how she was healed immediately. [48] And He said to her, "Daughter, be of good cheer; your faith has made you well. Go in peace."

Faith and your body

We may look at our family health history and assume that history is our destined future. It does not have to be this way. Just because everyone in your family has passed away from a specific disease or illness does not mean that you will too. Faith is powerful.

The woman with the issue of blood believed that if she touched the garments of Jesus, she would be made well. She walked up to Christ, pushing her way through the crowd for a touch of His garment. She took—perhaps stole—her healing, because she determined that no one would deny her health. She thought she could take her miracle without anyone, including Christ, knowing. She believed that His capacity to heal was endless, so no one would notice what she took. Christ discerned and stopped to explain what had transpired for our benefit, yet her recovery had already happened. Jesus confirmed that it was her faith, her belief put into action, that healed her, and He allowed her to go in peace.

We cannot come into contact with Jesus and then sneak away. In the partnership we have, God allows us to work with Him. We cannot obtain what He has to offer without faith. We have to nurture our measure of faith to receive the blessings He has to give. Get up and press forward. Claim your health in faith.

Pray

Heavenly Father, forgive me when I make assumptions about my destiny. Thank you for the measure of faith you have given to me. Help me to nurture it and boldly grab hold of the blessings you have for my health and my life. In Jesus' name, amen.

Read and Confess

Read: Matthew 13:32

Confess: The tiny amount of faith that I have is enough.

Delve Deeper

Are there any specifics that you need to change in the way you think about your body and your health?

_____
_____
_____
_____
_____
_____
_____
_____
_____
_____
_____
_____
_____
_____

Delve Deeper

What are some dreams you previously thought were unrealistic that you need to re-examine?

_____

Create
Create a healthy pantry.

Build a Habit
Go for a daily walk this week.

Put Faith into Action
Give a massage to a loved one.

WEEK 46
PAIN

Psalm 25:18

Look on my affliction and my pain, And forgive all my sins.

Pain

Will it hurt? As a dentist, people frequently ask me this question. No one wants to experience pain. Yet pain has a purpose. It is a protective mechanism that prevents us from continuing behavior that will cause injury. It is the body's alarm system to indicate that something is not functioning as it should. Pain prompts us to take action or make a change.

Many people seek dental treatment only when they are in pain. When they arrive at my office, they endure the pain of an injection in preparation for treatment. Sometimes there is pain after the treatment as the body works to heal itself. It's all part of the process. If you are experiencing pain, take it to Father God. Ask God for wisdom to address the situation. Ask Him to show you the root cause. Be prepared to act on the information you receive. Know that any pain we go through in this realm is temporary. God is with us and will bring us through.

As you await the manifestation of relief, be kind to yourself. Pain is exhausting. Therefore, give yourself the care that you need. Give yourself extra rest, extra attention, and extra nourishment to allow healing. God sees you; believe that He is faithful.

Pray

Father in Heaven, forgive my sins so that I can receive the healing you have to offer. Thank you for healing my physical body and keeping me free from discomfort. Help me go beyond the distraction and pain to hear you and act on the information you give me so that I can better do your will. In Jesus' name, amen.

Read and Confess

Read: Isaiah 54:17

Confess: No weapon formed against my health shall prosper.

Delve Deeper

How can you be more consistent with what's working for you currently in maintaining good health?

_____

_____

_____

_____

_____

_____

Delve Deeper

How does physical pain cause you to overreact in your thoughts, medications, or self-talk?

_____

_____

_____

_____

_____

Create

Create a relaxing focal point in your home.

Build a Habit

Practice daily relaxation techniques this week.

Put Faith into Action

Be peaceful. Don't allow pain to make you act aggressively.

WEEK 47
PHYSICAL FITNESS

1 Corinthians 9:26-27

Therefore I run thus: not with uncertainty. Thus I fight: not as one who beats the air. [27] But I discipline my body and bring it into subjection, lest, when I have preached to others, I myself should become disqualified.

Physical fitness

When a professional athlete is good, they do not have to talk about wrong calls or make excuses. Their skill in the field of play is such that a bad call will not affect the outcome of the game. We can similarly live our lives by letting our actions do the witnessing. We should be enthusiastic about exercising our physical body and keep our bodies in top condition. The effort helps to create ripple effects throughout the rest of our lives.

Physical fitness improves our techniques and increases our stamina. We learn to be quick on our feet. As we condition our bodies, our minds become mentally prepared. We will be able to maintain our independence longer. We will experience more energy to enjoy time with the children in our lives. The discipline we have with our bodies will spill over into other areas of our lives. Maintaining our body prepares us for our spiritual fight.

We live more fully for Christ when we invest in our bodies. The time spent results in an improved physical appearance as well as more energy. Non-Christians will see us as a better witness for Christ. Our body reflects our obedience and self-control. We can witness to others while enjoying the good life ourselves.

Pray

Dear Lord, forgive me when I'm careless about my health and fitness. Thank you for your Word, encouragement, and the ripple effects that come when I gain discipline in just a single area of my life. Help me to maintain my body so that I may be a better witness for you. In Jesus' name, amen.

Confess

I discipline my body as I witness for Christ.

Delve Deeper

In what area of your health do you excel?

_____
_____
_____
_____
_____
_____
_____

Delve Deeper

In what area of your health would you like to improve? How can you make that improvement a reality?

_____

_____

_____

_____

_____

Create

Create a shopping list of foods to nourish the temple of God.

Build a Habit

This week read the label before you buy anything at the grocery store.

Put Faith into Action

Prioritize your workouts this week.

WEEK 48
BOLDLY BREAK BREAD

1 Corinthians 11:27-30

Therefore whoever eats this bread or drinks this cup of the Lord in an unworthy manner will be guilty of the body and blood of the Lord. [28]But let a man examine himself, and so let him eat of the bread and drink of the cup. [29]For he who eats and drinks in an unworthy manner eats and drinks judgment to himself, not discerning the Lord's body. [30]For this reason many are weak and sick among you, and many sleep.

Boldly break bread

You have to eat. Eating is a daily necessity and fellowshipping with Christ is a daily necessity. Communion is the remembrance of the contract we have with God. A healthy body requires food, and a healthy spirit demands edification through the Word. Total health is yours through the body and blood of Christ. Boldness is your power, and you can dine at the Lord's Table with confidence.

You celebrate all the promises of life in Christ with communion.

You have the pledge of a healthy body and a healthy relationship with God. The act of communion means you can feast with Christ. Formally share yourself with Him to give thanksgiving and receive the gifts He has freely given to you. The act makes you remember to have gratitude and to do as Christ would do when you interact with others. Ask for forgiveness, and then receive it with the audacity of belief and not as a religious exercise. Communion is part of abiding in Christ. It helps you exist, proceed, and rest in Christ.

When you go boldly to the communion table, you can receive all that Christ died to give you. Christ endured a broken body to heal your physical body. Christ bled to forgive your sins. Accept the body and the blood of Christ boldly, and receive the benefits that it provides.

Pray

Heavenly Father, I confess that I do not always come to your table in an acceptable manner. Thank you for the gift of the body and blood of Christ for total healing of my body and spirit. Help me to conduct myself in a way to receive all the benefits Christ died to give me. In Jesus' name, amen.

Confess

I examine myself and confess my sins prior to receiving communion.

Delve Deeper

How are you different than you were five years ago?

_____

_____

_____

_____
_____
_____
_____
_____
_____
_____
_____
_____
_____
_____

Delve Deeper

In what ways are you good or bad at forgiveness?

_____
_____
_____
_____
_____
_____

Create
Create a go-to recipe using items that are always in your pantry.

Build a Habit
Try something new this week.

Put Faith into Action
Be quick to forgive yourself and others this week.

WEEK 49
NOTHING TO WEAR

Luke 12:22
Then He said to His disciples, "Therefore I say to you, do not worry about your life, what you will eat; nor about the body, what you will put on.

Nothing to wear

How many times do we stand in front of our closets and lament that we have nothing to wear? We believe our outfit will affect our progress in the world. A new season comes, and the media and mass marketers would have us believe our wardrobe is obsolete. All of this leads to disobedience because we have anxiety about what to wear.

We have a variety of solutions at our disposal. Perhaps we can add a few accessories and one major item and get through the season without being a total outcast or looking destitute or outdated. Events list the suggested attire to help us feel at ease. We try on various outfits to find the right choice. We may have multiple options lined up because things could change the day of the event due to our mood or our waistline due to bloating or anxiety.

Yet, this scripture goes beyond fashion. Inner beauty is the essence of this scripture. There is more to our appearance than the clothes we wear. The fashion icon Coco Channel said elegance does not consist in putting on a new dress. Christian women should carry themselves with grace as an example of Christ on earth. Let the radiance of being carefree in God's care be the attire the world sees.

Pray

Father in Heaven, I confess that I do worry about what to put on my body; please forgive me. Thank you for your love and care and the ability to walk clothed in your love. Let my inner beauty radiate out as a reflection of your love. In Jesus' name, amen.

Read and Confess

Read: Psalm 30:11
Confess: Thanks be to God, I am clothed with gladness.

Delve Deeper

If your body could talk, what would it tell you?

Delve Deeper
What makes a person look elegant, graceful or carefree?

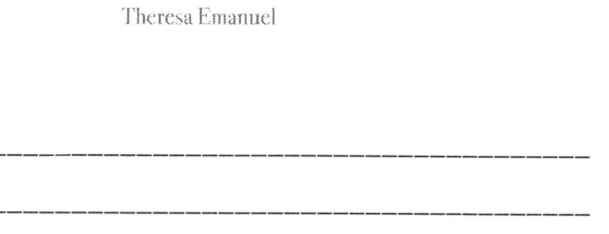

Create
Create an everyday makeup look.

Build a Habit
This month, shop without using credit cards.

Put Faith into Action
Set and keep a budget for your wardrobe this season.

WEEK 50
PROSPERITY OF THE BODY

3 John 1:2
Beloved, I pray that you may prosper in all things and be in health, just as your soul prospers.

Prosperity of the body

Without health, it is impossible to enjoy good fortune or relish the blessings that should be yours as a child of God. The saying, "healthy, wealthy, and wise" is no accident. Health comes first. Health makes it easier to function and enjoy life.

Have you been out with friends when you were sick? Cherished friends and venues are hard to enjoy when you're ill. Sickness depletes the body of vitality and enthusiasm. Well-being is necessary to be successful in your everyday life. Good health is difficult, if not impossible, to purchase. Care for and maintain your body. With good health comes energy for the activities of daily living. Diet, exercise, sleep, and stress management all play a part in allowing you to flourish physically.

You're feeding your soul with the Word of God. Your soul is supplied with the milk and meat of the Word to renew it and allow it to prosper. Feed your physical body the nutrients it needs to maintain health. As you rest in the knowledge of God, give your body the physical rest it needs. Knowing that your hope is in the Lord should allow you to manage stress. The prosperity of your soul will help you be in health.

Pray

Heavenly Father, forgive me when I take my health for granted. Thank you for the Word that helps my soul prosper. Help me to nourish my body so that it too will prosper and give you glory. In Jesus' name, amen.

Read and Confess

Read: Isaiah 57: 18-19
Confess: God heals me and gives me peace.

Delve Deeper

What does it mean to you to prosper in health?

_____
_____
_____
_____
_____
_____
_____
_____

Delve Deeper

What are you feeding your body to help it thrive?

_____

_____

_____

Create

What age do you equate with "old?" What does someone of that age look like? Is that who you want to be? Create a vision of the person you want to be at that age.

Build a Habit

Stretch each morning as soon as you get out of bed.

Put Faith into Action

Give yourself grace this week with downtime, extra rest or whatever your body needs to flourish.

WEEK 51
EXERCISE

1 Timothy 4:8

For bodily exercise profits a little, but godliness is profitable for all things, having promise of the life that now is and of that which is to come.

Exercise

Exercise versus godliness is an interesting comparison. When Paul wrote this scripture, people were much more active. When we read about the ministry of Jesus, He is walking almost everywhere He goes. I believe that Timothy knew very well the benefit of physical exercise, and Paul is saying how much more beneficial godliness is in comparison.

Today, I am not sure we all know what it feels like to be in excellent physical condition. Today, if walking up the stairs is too difficult, there is frequently an elevator or escalator nearby. If we do not have the strength to open a jar, we have a gadget to do it for us. Modern conveniences make it easy for an out-of-shape person to function in today's world. God wants better for us.

We should enjoy the little profit of bodily exercise. Exercise will keep our body healthy while helping us gain discipline. Physical conditioning will prevent laziness and improve self-control. If we keep our body in motion, it's easier to stay active. As we continue to exercise, our relationship with food will change because we will nourish our body for better performance. Exercise will enhance our mental outlook and our sleep. We should learn to exercise and push our body beyond what we think it can handle. Remember, we can do all things through Christ, including physical pursuits.

Pray

Heavenly Father, forgive me when I fail to gain the little profit that bodily exercise provides. Thank you for my body and my life in this world and the next. Help me to keep my body healthy so I may be a better servant for you. In Jesus' name, amen.

Read and Confess

Read: Romans 12:1

Confess: I exercise my body and offer it to God as a living sacrifice.

Delve Deeper

How do the duties of being a multifaceted Christian woman make you appreciate your physical mobility and health?

_____

_____

_____

_____

_____

Delve Deeper

How do your mind and body respond when you go a long time without exercising?

_____
_____
_____
_____
_____
_____
_____

Create
Create a morning routine.

Build a Habit
This week get up and stretch at least once every hour.

Put Faith into Action
This week, kneel when you say your evening prayers.

WEEK 52
AGE JOYFULLY

Proverbs 16:31
**The silver-haired head is a crown of glory,
If it is found in the way of righteousness.**

Age joyfully

We want time to pass so that we can progress, but we do not desire the effects of time to show on our physical bodies. The world burdens women with a demand to remain eternally beautiful and then defines beauty as that of youth. God defines beauty differently. According to God, beauty comes from within; it is the reflection of a spirit that is gentle and quiet and loves the Lord. Sadly, our pride wants a fallen world to appreciate our beauty.

When I started getting gray hair, more than one of my patients commented. Even though I assured them I was worthy, I got shaking heads of disapproval and the verbal chastisement of people saying I was too young for gray hair. People judge our appearance before we open our mouths. Then that judgment extends to our message or offer. The story of Sara shows that age doesn't matter to God. He will still use you to fulfill His purpose.

Let's extend our faith to our outward appearance. A life with Christ should be anti-aging. Those who age better avoid negativity, stress, and excess. The Word gives us the solution to stress and negativity. The Bible also cautions against excess while encouraging eating well, resting well, and exercising. Embrace God's definition of beauty and obey the Word. You'll be beautiful inside and out.

Pray

Heavenly Father, forgive me when I fall captive of the world's definition of beauty. Thank you for making me beautiful from within. Help me to trust you and to be obedient to your Word so that I may maintain my physical appearance as you instruct. In Jesus' name, amen.

Read and Confess

Read: 1 Peter 3:3-4

Confess: I have the incorruptible beauty of a gentle and quiet spirit.

Delve Deeper

What is old age and what is its purpose?

_____
_____
_____
_____
_____
_____

Delve Deeper
What does legacy mean and what legacy do you want to leave?

_____
_____
_____
_____
_____

Create

Create a flower arrangement. Kindly share a picture of it by tagging me on Instagram @p31virtues.

Build a Habit

Make your bed every day this week.

Put Faith into Action

Visit someone who doesn't get out much.

CONCLUSION

CONCLUSION

Congratulations on completing the 52 weeks of this devotional study! I'm sure you've come a long way in your faith, relationships, and all aspects of your busy life. You have studied, prayed, and reflected through journaling. You are now able to navigate the natural world from a place of spiritual peace and calm. By nurturing every part of your tripartite nature, it is easier to ensure that your thoughts and actions are Word driven. I trust that your creative pursuits have made your life more relaxing and beautiful while enriching the lives of others. As you continue to put your faith into action daily, your multiple facets will glow brighter.

If we haven't been in touch yet, please email theresa@p31virtues.com and let me know what habits you have developed that have had the most impact on your life. Frequently visit calm.p31virtues.com for updated bonus material and information on how we can connect. Continue to abide, ask, affirm, and act according to God's Word. The journey lasts a lifetime. Enjoy it from a place of calm and peace.

Blessings,
Theresa

ABOUT THE AUTHOR

ABOUT THE AUTHOR

Theresa Emanuel is the creator of the @P31Virtues Christian Lifestyle Brand found on Instagram, Facebook, Pinterest, and Twitter. As an author and speaker, she encourages Christian women to put their faith into action harnessing spiritual laws to exponentially increase joy and good success. Using her life experiences from serving as a United States Air Force Officer to gaining her Doctorate of Dental Surgery, Theresa shares wisdom on the impact of spiritual laws regardless of time, circumstances, location, or leadership level. She is the author of *It's All About Food: Lessons in Fellowshipping Daily with Christ*, in which she shares the simplicity and joy of inviting Christ into every aspect of life. In this way, Theresa is an insightful personal stylist of the heart, exuding the love of God, and brilliantly relating how her faith influences her multifaceted life. Her honest storytelling encourages readers to seek God's best for their lives while clearly delivering perceptive action steps to make that life a reality. Visit the author online at www.p31virtues.com.

Made in the USA
Columbia, SC
16 March 2021